CAKES

Galore

CAKES
Galore

Valerie Barrett

spruce

An Hachette UK Company
www.hachette.co.uk

First published in Great Britain in 2006 by Spruce,
a division of Octopus Publishing Group Ltd
Endeavour House
189 ShaftesburyAvenue
London
WC2H 8JY
www.octopusbooks.co.uk
www.octopusbooksusa.com

This edition published in 2013

Distributed in the US by
Hachette Book Group USA
237 Park Avenue
New York NY 10017 USA

Distributed in Canada by
Canadian Manda Group
165 Dufferin Street
Toronto, Ontario, Canada M6K 3H6

ISBN 978-1-84601-447-5

A CIP catalogue record for this book is available
from the British Library

Printed and bound in China

10 9 8 7 6 5 4 3 2 1

CONTENTS

INTRODUCTION

Few can resist the temptation of a slice of
home-made cake, whether it's the simplest
jam-filled sponge or an elaborate, layered and
fancily decorated creation. Important in many countries and cultures,
cakes are often the centrepiece on special occasions.

★ AN ANCIENT CRAFT ★

The first cakes were made when primitive people
discovered how to make flour. The earliest known
examples, discovered by archaeologists in the remains
of Neolithic villages, were made from crushed grains,
moistened, sweetened with honey and cooked on a hot
stone. For centuries, baking remained a very haphazard
affair because it was difficult to control heat. The
Ancient Egyptians were the first to develop reliable
cooking methods and ovens and evidence of the cakes
they made can be seen in their tomb paintings. The
Romans were also skilled bakers and learnt to leaven
their cake mixtures with yeast.

The word 'cake' is Anglo Saxon in origin and has
been around for centuries, but it's meaning has
changed over time. In Medieval times, a cake was any
item that could be shaped into a small round patty –
we still refer to a 'cake' of soap and 'fishcakes'. Later,
the word was used for small unsweetened breads.
Eventually cakes became distinct from savoury items
and were usually yeast-leavened combinations of flour,
nuts, dried fruits and honey that resembled what we
now know as 'tea cakes' and 'tea breads'.

During the Renaissance, Italian cooks, famed for
their baking skills, were employed in households in
England and France. They introduced the forerunner to

the sponge cake – a thin crisp cake, lightened by eggs and sugar whisked to a thick frothy mixture. By the mid-18th century, yeast had been largely replaced as a raising agent by this whisked-egg method. The mixture was poured into metal or wooden moulds, which, though often very elaborate, were sometimes just plain tin hoops set on a baking sheet. It is from these hoops that our modern cake tins evolved.

Initially, cakes were served as in-between-meal snacks with sweet wine. Elaborate cakes would often be made for displaying at banquets, but were rarely eaten; the idea of serving cake as a dessert didn't occur until the mid-19th century when 'Service à la Russe' became fashionable. In richer households, the meal was served by servants, and diners were brought individual dishes one course at a time. At last dessert had been invented.

Gradually, baking ingredients became more readily available due to mass production and better transportation and modern leavening agents, such as baking soda and baking powder, completely changed cake-making. The Victorians developed ovens with more reliable temperature control and the Victoria sandwich cake became a familiar tea-time treat. A few decades later, baking became a vital skill for young women: a 'good' housewife was judged on her ability to bake cakes as well as prepare meals and clean!

After World War II, pre-packaged cake mixes were introduced as 'time-savers' in American grocery stores by companies such as 'Betty Crocker'. At first, the powdered mixture didn't sell well and it was discovered that housewives felt guilty using a product that was simply mixed with water. When the recipe was changed so that it needed an egg as well, sales rocketed and packet cake mixes became available all over the world.

★ CAKE-MAKING TODAY ★

The massive range and easily availability of ingredients and equipment have simplified cake-making, and the popularity of home-baking has risen. Easy travel and communication has increased our knowledge of cakes from around the world so that today we are as likely to make a Turkish semolina and sesame cake as we are a date and walnut loaf. This book contains a wonderful selection of cakes, from all-time classics to more contemporary recipes, to suit every occasion, whether you are a novice or an experienced baker.

DIFFERENT WAYS OF
Making Cakes

There are five standard methods of cake-making: creaming, all-in-one, whisking, rubbing-in and melting.

★ CREAMING ★

This is probably the most traditional method of cake-making – the Victoria sandwich is made by this method. The fat and sugar are beaten together until the mixture is light in colour and fluffy in texture, indicating that a large amount of air has been incorporated. Further air is trapped when eggs are beaten in. Sifted flour is then gently folded into the mixture. During baking, the fat melts and the raising agent reacts with the liquid in the eggs to produce carbon dioxide. This, together with the trapped air, makes the cake rise.

All ingredients, especially butter and eggs, must be at room temperature, or the cake will not rise properly. (Soften butter in the microwave on low power for 10–15 seconds if you've forgotten to take it out of the fridge.)

★ ALL-IN-ONE ★

Also known as a 'one-stage' sponge, this is made with the same ingredients and in the same proportions as a Victoria sandwich. The texture will be more open and less fine than a traditional creamed cake, but this method is much quicker and easier. Because the ingredients are not added gradually, there will be insufficient air in the cake for a really good rise, so additional baking powder is used in combination with self-raising flour. Beat the ingredients together for two minutes only, if you are making it by hand, or one minute if you are using a hand-held electric mixer. It is particularly important, with this method, to bake the cake immediately after mixing it because the baking powder will already be activated.

★ WHISKING ★

Whisked sponges are the lightest of cakes and often contain no added fat and only a small amount of flour. The eggs and sugar are whisked together for at least 10 minutes, until the mixture has roughly tripled in volume, is very pale and the whisk leaves a 'ribbon' trail on top of the mixture when lifted out of the bowl. Often the mixture is initially whisked over hot water to dissolve the sugar, then further whisked until it has cooled. A huge amount of air is incorporated at this stage and no further raising agent is needed. Finally, sifted flour, and sometimes other dry ingredients, such as unsweetened cocoa powder or ground nuts, are folded in with a large metal spoon to ensure that as little as possible of the precious air is lost.

A classic whisked sponge is made without butter and stays fresh for only a day or two. It has a light, airy, even texture. A Genoese sponge, which is made in the same way, usually has a slightly higher proportion of sugar. After folding in the flour, a little melted butter, margarine or oil is trickled down the side of the bowl and gently stirred in. This makes a moister cake and improves the flavour and keeping quantities. A Swiss roll can be made from either type of whisked sponge; the addition of a spoonful of warm water will prevent the sponge from cracking as it is rolled into shape.

★ RUBBING IN ★

This method is used for cakes that are typically made with half, or less than half, fat to flour and gives a fairly open texture. It is often used for light fruit cakes and tea-loaves. The fat is cut into small pieces, then rubbed into the flour with the fingertips until the mixture resembles fine breadcrumbs, then the remaining ingredients are stirred in. The butter should be cold and firm, but not too hard, so take it out of the fridge about 10 minutes before you need it.

★ MELTING ★

Often used for moist cakes, such as gingerbread and fruit cake, the fat, sugar, syrup and sometimes fruit are all gently heated in a saucepan over the hob until just melted. The mixture is usually cooled before the eggs and remaining dry ingredients are stirred in. Fat should be at room temperature and cut it into small pieces so that it melts before other ingredients are over-heated.

EQUIPMENT

You don't need a vast amount of equipment to make a cake: measuring equipment, a bowl, wooden spoon and cake tin are the only essentials, but there are a huge range of items that make baking a cake even easier.

★ MEASURES ★

The success of a cake depends on the ingredients being in the correct proportions, so a set of accurate measuring spoons, weighing scales or cups and a calibrated, easy-to-read measuring jug are all vital. Kitchen scales can be electronic, balance-based or spring-operated.

Electronic scales allow you to weigh out ingredients to the nearest gram and many have an add-and-weigh system so you can reset the display to zero and weigh the second ingredient on top of the first. Take particular care when measuring raising agents: over-fill the spoon first, then level the top with the back of a knife.

★ BOWLS ★

Whether glass, ceramic or stainless steel, a set of different-sized, heat-proof bowls for mixing, beating and melting ingredients is invaluable for cake-making.

If possible, choose deep bowls for cake mixing rather than wide shallow ones.

★ SIFTER ★

Invest in at least two strong, fine stainless-steel or plastic sieves; a larger one for sifting dry ingredients, such as flour, to remove any lumps and make it more aerated and easier to mix, and a small one for sifting icing sugar over the tops of baked cakes.

★ SPATULA ★

A flexible plastic or rubber spatula can be used to scrape the last little bit of cake mixture from the bowl and for smoothing the top of the cake level before baking. It is also useful for folding delicate ingredients, such as whisked egg whites, into cake mixtures.

★ WHISKS ★

Food processors and mixers are excellent for creaming butter and sugar together, whisking eggs and sugar to a thick foam and for beating egg whites. You should,

however, always fold in dry ingredients by hand to avoid over-mixing the cake batter. Hand-held electric mixers can be used in the same way, but are more convenient because they allow you to control the movement around the bowl. They can also be used in a bowl over a pan of near-boiling water when making whisked sponges. Wire balloon whisks and hand-held rotary whisks are good, but more time-consuming, alternatives.

★ TINS ★

These are available in all sorts of shapes and sizes, from round and square tins and rectangular loaf pans to

petal-, heart- and novelty-shaped ones. Look for tins made from heavy-gauge metal; the thicker the gauge the less likely they are to warp or have hot spots. Aluminium is inexpensive, simple to clean and responds well to changes in heat. It does however, dent easily, so treat it carefully, or, if you can afford it, choose anodised aluminium. Tin is also a good metal for bakeware, but it will rust unless thoroughly dried after use. Non-stick tins are excellent and make turning out cakes much easier; again, they need careful use and storage as they scratch easily. If you use pans with a dark non-stick lining, you may need to reduce the oven temperature slightly as dark colours absorb heat. Loose-bottomed tins simplify turning out cakes. You can also buy 'spring-release' cake tins, which open out, so that the sides of the tin can simply be lifted off the

cake and base. They are invaluable for delicate cakes, which should not normally be inverted after baking.

★ BAKING SHEETS ★

These can be used in combination with cake hoops and novelty cake tins without bases. They may be entirely flat or have a lip along the length of one side. Baking trays have a lip all around the edge. It is vital to choose good-quality, heavy ones, which won't distort at high temperature. For cake-making, avoid baking sheets that are very dark as they absorb more heat, which means that the base of the cake will burn more easily. (Dark sheets are intended for other kinds of cooking, such as baking bread.)

★ SUGAR THERMOMETER ★

This is the most reliable way to check the temperature of a boiling sugar syrup when making caramel or frostings such as crème au beurre.

★ TIMER ★

This is essential, particularly for light sponges and roulades, as even an extra couple of minutes in the oven can result in a dry, over-cooked cake. Most modern ovens have a timer, but a hand-held digital or rotating dial timer is useful, particularly if you want to go into another room while your cake is baking.

★ WIRE RACK ★

The best way to cool all cakes, whether they are turned out of their tins straight away or left to cool partially or completely in their tins, is to rest them on a wire rack. This allows air to circulate, so that the cake cools quickly and prevents trapped warmth, which would make the base soggy.

★ PIPING BAGS AND NOZZLES ★

These are useful for piping whipped cream, frostings, icing and melted chocolate onto cakes to decorate them. Most piping bags are now made of nylon; the best are glued and double stitched along the seams to prevent splitting or leakage. You can also buy disposable plastic piping bags.

★ AIRTIGHT CONTAINERS ★

Because home-made cakes do not contain preservatives, they should be stored in an airtight tin or plastic container as soon as they are cool to keep them fresh. Cheesecake types and those covered with butter-based icing or cream topping, or containing ingredients such as fresh fruit, should be stored in the fridge.

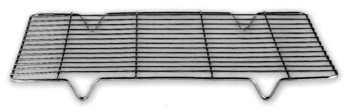

INGREDIENTS

Most cakes are made from just a few basics: flour, sugar, eggs and usually butter, plus some flavouring ingredients, whether just a few drops of pure vanilla extract or a mixture of juicy fruits and nuts. Whatever your choice, always use good-quality, fresh ingredients to ensure that you make the best cakes.

★ FLOUR ★

Most cakes are made with soft wheat flour, either plain or, more often, self-raising, which has added raising agents. Because flour contains gluten, it is important not to beat the cake mixture too much after adding the flour, as doing so will develop the gluten, giving the cake a tough texture. Always check the 'use-by' date on flour, as raising agents deteriorate and your cake may not rise as well. Wholemeal flour is milled from the whole wheat kernel. It is much coarser and heavier than white flour and gives cakes a denser, more filling texture. Some supermarkets sell 'sponge flour', which is a self-raising flour finely milled from especially soft wheat.

★ RAISING AGENTS ★

Raising agents are sometimes used in addition to self-raising flour, particularly in all-in-one mixtures where less air will be beaten into the cake mixture. Don't be tempted to add more than the recipe states or your cake will rise rapidly, then sink unevenly when removed from the oven, and the taste will be adversely affected. Baking powder is a mixture of cream of tartar and bicarbonate of soda and releases carbon dioxide bubbles when it comes into contact with a liquid. Bicarbonate of soda needs an acid ingredient as well as liquid to be activated. It is occasionally used in cakes that contain citrus juice, buttermilk or yoghurt.

★ EGGS ★

Eggs add richness to cakes and create volume. Size really matters: most of the recipes in this book use medium eggs, unless stated otherwise. Always use eggs at room temperature when making cakes, as cold eggs may curdle and cold egg whites produce less volume when whisked. Eggs will absorb flavours from other foods, so they should be kept in their box or a separate compartment in the fridge and stored pointed end downwards, which helps to prevent moisture in the egg evaporating.

★ BUTTER ★

Butter, either salted or unsalted adds moistness, colour and flavour to a whole range of cakes. When using in creamed mixtures, it should always be soft, but not melting, so that it can be successfully combined with the sugar. Salted butter will keep well in the fridge for up to a month, unsalted for just two weeks, but both can be frozen for up to 6 months.

★ OTHER FATS ★

'Hard' block margarine can be used as an alternative to butter in most recipes, and is less expensive, although it doesn't have the same creamy taste. Soft-tub margarine is often used in all-in-one mixtures as it can be used straight from the fridge and blends quickly and easily. Avoid using low-fat margarines and spreads in cake-making as they have a high water content.

★ SUGAR ★

There are many different types of sugar used in cake-making, each with its own distinct characteristics. Granulated sugar has large granules and, in baking, is mostly used for sprinkling over cakes as a crunchy topping, as is demerara sugar, which has a deep golden colour. Caster sugar has fine grains and is most commonly used for cake-making as it creams beautifully with butter, trapping lots of air. Golden caster sugar is

the unrefined version and has a pale gold colour. Icing sugar is a fine powdered sugar, mostly used in cake icings and frostings as it mixes to perfect smoothness. Soft light and dark brown sugars refer to any fine moist brown sugar made from a combination of refined sugar and a small amount of molasses to darken, flavour and colour. Muscovado sugar, also known as Barbados sugar, is unrefined 'raw' cane sugar and may be light or dark. It is usually finely grained and gives cakes a rich flavour and dark colour. There are many other sweeteners used in cakes, including golden syrup, maple syrup, honey, molasses and malt extract.

★ FRUIT AND NUTS ★

Both fresh and dried fruits are used in cakes, either folded into the mixture or for decorating the top. When fruit is dried, the flavour and sweetness is intensified, so recipes containing a large amount of dried fruit often contain less sugar to compensate. Adding dried fruit does not affect the moisture of the mixture, so you can usually substitute one type of dried fruit for another in a recipe. Always use good-quality, plump moist dried fruit for the best flavour.

★ CHOCOLATE ★

Chocolate is a popular cake flavouring and it is vital to use one with a high percentage of cocoa solids – 70% or more is ideal. Unsweetened cocoa powder is a dark bitter powder than can be substituted for the same quantity of flour in many recipes. Avoid using drinking chocolate, unless specified by the recipe, as it contains only about 25% cocoa powder, the remainder being sugar.

★ ALCOHOL ★

Spirits, such as rum and brandy, sherry and liqueurs are sometimes added to cake mixtures in small quantities to flavour them and they can also be used to soak dried fruit before adding it to cakes. The alcohol will evaporate during baking, leaving a subtle taste behind. Some cakes are sprinkled with alcohol after baking, which gives a stronger flavour.

★ SPICES AND FLAVOURINGS ★

Ground dried spices, most commonly cinnamon and ginger, feature in many cake recipes. Vanilla is also popular and is used in combination with many other flavourings including chocolate. Citrus zest, especially orange and lemon, is another great flavouring for cakes: use unwaxed fruit if possible.

TROUBLESHOOTING

All the recipes in this book have foolproof, step-by-step instructions to help ensure your cakes are perfect every time. However, occasionally problems do occur, and it's important to find out what went wrong and why, so you can avoid the same mistake next time.

Q – *I haven't got a tin in the right size. Is it okay to use one slightly bigger or smaller?*

A – For the best results, always use the tin size recommended in your chosen recipe as it may not bake successfully in a tin that is markedly different in size. It's not a good idea to use a smaller tin as the mixture may overflow. Sometimes you can use a slightly larger tin, but remember to adjust the cooking time if you do so, as the mixture will be shallower and will cook much faster. If you don't have a big selection of tins, it may be worth investing in a 'multi-size' cake tin, which can be adjusted to the size you require. If you want to bake a round cake instead of a square one, or vice versa, an 18cm round is the equivalent of a 15cm square and a 23cm round the equivalent of a 20cm square.

Q – *I need a cake for a special occasion in a few months time. What sort of cake would be best to make in advance and how should I store it?*

A – Sponges made with the creaming method, such as a Victoria sponge cake, can be covered with fondant icing and will keep well for up to a week if wrapped in foil and kept in a clean airtight tin or plastic container. Alternatively, you can freeze an undecorated sponge for up to a month. If you want a cake that can be made well ahead, choose a rich fruit cake. This should be made two to three months before you decorate it to allow the cake to mature; its keeping qualities will improve further if you brush the top with alcohol, such as brandy or rum. After baking the cake, make sure it is completely cold, then wrap it in a double layer of greaseproof paper, then in foil.

Q – *I'm never quite sure when to take my cake out of the oven. How can I tell whether it's properly cooked or not?*
A – To test a baked sponge, press the centre gently with a fingertip; it should feel spongy and give very slightly, then rise immediately, leaving no impression. A whisked sponge should be just shrinking away from the sides of the tin. To test a fruit cake, insert a fine skewer into the centre, leave it for 5 seconds, then remove. It should come away cleanly; if any mixture is sticking to the skewer, bake it for a little longer.

Q – *Whenever I make a sponge cake and add the eggs to the creamed butter and sugar mixture, it curdles. Does this matter and how can I prevent it?*
A – If the creamed mixture curdles when you add the eggs, some of the air you've carefully beaten in will be lost and your cake won't rise quite as well. All the ingredients must be at room temperature before you start. If your kitchen is cold, stand the butter and sugar over a bowl of warm water for a few minutes, then place the bowl of beaten eggs over the water while you cream the butter and sugar. Add the beaten eggs a little at a time, beating thoroughly after each addition. If you see the mixture start to separate, beat in a spoonful of sifted flour before adding the rest of the eggs.

Q – *My sponge cakes always look perfect when I take them out of the oven, but stick to the tin when I try to turn them out, no matter how well I grease them. What am I doing wrong?*
A – It's really disheartening when you damage your cake trying to remove it from the tin. For most cakes, you will need to line the tin with baking parchment – either just the base or the sides too – even if the tin is a non-stick one. If you use greaseproof paper, you may need to brush it lightly with oil or melted and cooled unsalted butter. Once removed from the oven, whisked sponges should be turned out straight away, but all other cakes benefit from being left in the tin for a few minutes to firm up and to allow the cake to shrink slightly from the sides. Some, such as rich fruit cakes, can be left in the tin until completely cool – each recipe will give advice on this. To remove the cake, run a palette knife around the edge of the tin. Turn out the cake onto a wire cooling rack covered with a clean tea towel, remove the lining paper, then cover the cake with another cooling rack. Invert both racks together and remove the top rack. Loose-bottomed cake tins make removal considerably easier, but don't use them for very wet mixtures or upside-down cakes, or some of the mixture may seep out during baking.

GRANDMA'S
FAVOURITES

MISSISSIPPI MUD Cake

Top-quality chocolate will bring out the best in this rich and tempting chocolate and nut extravaganza.

MAKES: 8–10 SLICES

250g butter, softened
250g caster sugar
3 eggs, beaten
115g dark bitter chocolate, melted
1 teaspoon vanilla extract
225g plain flour
4 tablespoons unsweetened cocoa
   powder
½ teaspoon baking powder
Pinch of salt
100g pecans, chopped

FOR THE ICING
125g unsalted butter, softened
55g icing sugar
150g dark bitter chocolate, melted
Mini chocolate curls, for decorating

1. Preheat the oven to 180°C/350°F/Gas mark 4. Grease a round-ended 30 x 11cm loaf tin (or a 23cm bundt or ring tin).

2. For the cake, cream the butter and sugar together in a bowl until pale and fluffy, then gradually beat in the eggs. Add the melted chocolate and vanilla extract and mix well.

3. Sift the flour, cocoa powder, baking powder and salt over the chocolate mixture and fold in with the chopped pecans. Spoon the mixture into the prepared tin and level the surface.

4. Bake in the oven for 40–45 minutes, or until a skewer inserted into the centre comes out clean. Cool in the tin for 10 minutes, then turn out onto a wire rack and leave to cool completely.

5. To make the icing, beat the butter in a bowl until pale and fluffy. Beat in the icing sugar, then stir in the melted chocolate, mixing well. Place the cake on a serving plate, flat-base up, and spread with the chocolate icing. Sprinkle mini chocolate curls along the centre and serve in slices.

CAKE TIP
Alternatively, try using chopped walnuts or a variety of chocolate chips instead of the pecans if preferred.

LAVENDER MADEIRA Cake

This is a buttery cake with a lovely, scented, summer flavour. Make sure the lavender is fresh and unsprayed.

MAKES: 8–10 SLICES

3 sprigs of fresh lavender, each about 10cm long
175g unsalted butter, softened
175g caster sugar
Finely grated zest of 1 lemon
3 eggs, beaten
225g self-raising flour

FOR THE ICING
4 tablespoons milk
3 sprigs of fresh lavender, each about 10cm long
175g icing sugar, sifted
Lavender food colouring (optional)
Extra small sprigs of fresh lavender, for decoration

1. Preheat the oven to 180°C/350°F/Gas mark 4. Grease and base line a deep 20cm round cake tin.

2. For the cake, remove the lavender flowers from the stalks; discard the stalks. Beat the butter and sugar together in a bowl until pale and fluffy. Add the lavender flowers, lemon zest, eggs and flour and beat until smooth, well mixed and creamy.

3. Turn the mixture into the prepared tin and level the surface. Bake in the oven for 30 minutes, then reduce the oven temperature to 170°C/325°F/Gas mark 3 and bake for a further 15–25 minutes, or until a skewer inserted into the centre comes out clean. Cool in the tin for 5 minutes, then turn out onto a wire rack and leave to cool completely.

4. To make the icing, put the milk and lavender sprigs in a very small saucepan. Bring just to the boil, then remove the pan from the heat. Cover and leave to stand for about 20 minutes. Strain the infused milk into a bowl and leave until cold.

5. Put the icing sugar in a bowl and mix in just enough flavoured milk (1–2 tablespoons) to make a thick coating consistency. Add a few drops of food colouring, if you like. Spread the icing evenly over the cake and decorate with small sprigs of fresh lavender. Serve in slices.

RHUBARB & GINGER Cake

Banish the blues with this warming and delicious cake. The cornmeal adds an
interesting texture and colour to this cake, but ground almonds could be used instead.

MAKES: 8–10 SLICES

200g plain flour
2 teaspoons baking powder
$\frac{1}{4}$ teaspoon salt
80g cornmeal or instant polenta
2 eggs
3 tablespoons milk
1 teaspoon vanilla extract
125g unsalted butter or margarine,
   softened
125g caster sugar
450g fresh rhubarb, trimmed and cut
   into chunks
3 tablespoons sliced (drained)
   preserved stem ginger

FOR THE TOPPING
75g plain flour
30g ground hazelnuts
5 tablespoons soft light brown sugar
$\frac{1}{2}$ teaspoon ground ginger
50g unsalted butter, diced
Sifted icing sugar, for dusting
Vanilla ice cream, crème fraîche or
   custard, to serve

1. Preheat the oven to 170°C/325°F/Gas mark 3. Grease and base line a
23cm springform tin fitted with a flat base.

2. For the cake, sift the flour, baking powder and salt into a bowl. Stir in
the cornmeal or polenta. Whisk the eggs in a separate bowl until thick,
pale and creamy and stir in the milk and vanilla extract.

3. In another bowl, cream the butter or margarine and sugar together
until pale and fluffy. Fold in the dry ingredients alternately with the
whisked egg mixture to make a thick batter.

4. Spoon the mixture into the prepared tin and level the surface. Arrange
the rhubarb and stem ginger on top.

5. To make the topping, mix the flour, ground hazelnuts, brown sugar and
ginger in a bowl. Rub in the butter until the mixture resembles coarse
crumbs. Sprinkle the topping mixture evenly over the rhubarb and stem
ginger so that some pieces of rhubarb are quite thickly coated, while
others are just dusted with the mixture.

6. Bake in the oven for 1–1$\frac{1}{4}$ hours, or until the cake is firm to the touch
and the crumb topping is golden. Test to ensure the rhubarb is tender by
gently inserting a skewer into one of the exposed pieces.

7. Cool in the tin for 5 minutes, then remove the sides of the tin and
transfer the cake to a serving plate. Dust with sifted icing sugar and serve
warm in slices with ice cream, crème fraîche or custard.

RUM Cake

This cake can double as a dessert. Serve it warm with pan-fried
bananas and vanilla ice cream for a sensational finish to a meal.

MAKES: 10–12 SLICES

200g unsalted butter, softened
250g soft light brown sugar
2 eggs, beaten
250g plain flour
½ teaspoon baking powder
1 teaspoon ground allspice
Pinch of salt
3 tablespoons dark rum

FOR THE TOPPING

50g caster sugar
3 tablespoons rum
40g unsalted butter

CAKE TIP
*This cake will freeze well.
Simply cut into slices and
wrap individually – that way
you can take them out as and
when needed. Perfect for
lunchboxes and picnics.*

1. Preheat the oven to 180°C/350°F/Gas mark 4. Grease and base line a 900g loaf tin.

2. For the cake, beat the butter in a bowl until pale and creamy, then add the sugar and beat for a further 3–4 minutes.

3. Gradually add the eggs, beating well after each addition. Sift the flour, baking powder, allspice and salt over the creamed mixture and fold in together with the rum.

4. Spoon the mixture into the prepared tin and level the surface. Bake in the oven for 50–55 minutes, or until the cake is firm to the touch and a skewer inserted into the centre comes out clean.

5. Meanwhile, make the topping. Place the sugar, rum, butter and 2 tablespoons of water in a saucepan and heat gently, stirring until the sugar has dissolved.

6. Remove the cake from the oven. Using a cocktail stick, prick the top of the cake lightly, then pour over the rum syrup. Cool in the tin for 10–15 minutes, then turn out and serve warm or cold in slices.

PASSION Cake

A thick, indulgent layer of sweet, soft cheese icing makes this cake extra special. Walnuts can be substituted for the pecans, if you like.

MAKES: 8 SQUARES

150ml safflower or sunflower oil
175g soft light brown sugar
3 eggs, beaten
½ teaspoon ground cinnamon
½ teaspoon freshly grated nutmeg
150g carrots, coarsely grated
1 banana, peeled and mashed
50g pecans, chopped
250g plain flour, sifted
1 tablespoon baking powder

FOR THE ICING
160g cream cheese or full-fat
   soft cheese, softened
100g icing sugar, sifted
Finely grated zest of ½ orange
50g pecans, chopped (optional)

1. Preheat the oven to 180°C/350°F/Gas mark 4. Grease and base line a deep 20cm square cake tin.

2. Put all the cake ingredients into a large mixing bowl and beat together until well mixed.

3. Spoon the mixture into the prepared tin and level the surface. Bake in the oven for 45–50 minutes, or until golden and a skewer inserted into the centre comes out clean.

4. Cool in the tin for 10 minutes, then turn out onto a wire rack and leave to cool completely.

5. Make the icing. Beat the cream cheese or soft cheese, icing sugar and orange zest together in a bowl until pale and fluffy. Spread the icing over the top of the cake and sprinkle with pecans before serving, if you like.

Cut into squares to serve.

BURNT-SUGAR Cake

MAKES: 8–10 SLICES

450g caster sugar
125ml boiling water
175g unsalted butter, softened
3 eggs, beaten
300g self-raising flour
1 teaspoon bicarbonate of soda
200ml soured cream

FOR THE ICING & DECORATION
125g unsalted butter, softened
250g icing sugar, sifted
3 tablespoons caster sugar

CAKE TIP
When making the caramel syrup, use a long-handled spoon to add the boiling water to the melted sugar – and be very careful as the liquid will bubble fiercely.

1. To make the caramel syrup, cook 200g of the sugar over medium heat in a medium, heavy-based saucepan, stirring occasionally until the sugar has melted. Cook, without stirring, until dark golden. Remove from the heat and carefully and gradually add the boiling water. Return the pan to the heat and simmer, stirring, for about 1 minute until the caramel has dissolved. Pour the caramel into a heat-proof measuring jug and set aside.

2. Preheat the oven to 180°C/350°F/Gas mark 4. Grease and base line two 20cm round sandwich cake tins.

3. Cream the butter and remaining sugar together in a bowl until pale and fluffy, then gradually beat in the eggs. In a separate bowl, sift together the flour and bicarbonate of soda. In another bowl, mix together the soured cream and 125ml of the cooled caramel syrup.

4. Fold the flour and caramel mixtures into the creamed mixture until well combined. Divide the mixture evenly between the prepared tins and level the surface. Bake in the oven for about 30 minutes, or until risen, golden brown and firm to the touch. Turn out onto a wire rack and leave to cool.

5. To make the icing, beat the butter in a bowl until creamy, then gradually stir in the icing sugar until combined. Add the remaining caramel syrup, mixing well. Sandwich the two cakes together with some icing, then spread the remaining icing over the top of the cake.

6. To make the decoration, lightly oil a baking sheet. Put the caster sugar into a small non-stick frying pan and heat gently until the mixture turns a golden colour, then pour it onto the prepared baking sheet. Leave until cold, then break the caramel into pieces and use to decorate the cake.

BUTTERMILK Cake

A light-tasting, simple cake that's incredibly easy to make and delicious to eat.

MAKES: 18 SLICES

175g unsalted butter, softened
300g caster sugar
300ml buttermilk
1 teaspoon vanilla extract
275g self-raising flour
1 teaspoon baking powder
½ teaspoon bicarbonate of soda
Pinch of salt
4 egg whites

CAKE TIP

If you can't get hold of buttermilk, use 150ml of milk mixed with 150ml of plain yoghurt.

1. Preheat the oven to 180°C/350°F/gas mark 4. Grease and base line a 28 x 20 x 4cm cake tin or baking tin.

2. Cream the butter and sugar together in a bowl with 1 tablespoon of the buttermilk and the vanilla extract.

3. Sift the flour, baking powder, bicarbonate of soda and salt together three times into a separate bowl. Stir the flour mixture and remaining buttermilk alternately into the creamed mixture, until well combined.

4. In a separate bowl, whisk the egg whites until stiff. Add one-third of the whisked egg whites to the sponge mixture to lighten it, then gently fold in the rest.

5. Pour the mixture evenly into the prepared tin. Bake in the oven for 35–40 minutes, or until just firm to the touch. Cool in the tin for 5 minutes, then turn out onto a wire rack and leave to cool completely. Serve in slices.

DARK JAMAICAN GINGER Cake

Ginger has been grown in Jamaica since 1547. This cake uses freshly grated root ginger in place of ground ginger, resulting in a deliciously moist cake with a wonderful mellow aroma.

MAKES: 10–12 SLICES

225g plain flour
2 teaspoons baking powder
½ teaspoon bicarbonate of soda
1 teaspoon ground allspice
½ teaspoon freshly grated nutmeg
225g unsalted butter
125g soft light brown sugar
2 tablespoons grated peeled fresh
   root ginger
125ml evaporated milk
125g black treacle or molasses
2 eggs, beaten

1. Preheat the oven to 180°C/350°F/Gas mark 4. Grease and line a 900g loaf tin.

2. Sift the flour, baking powder, bicarbonate of soda, allspice and nutmeg into a bowl. Add the butter and rub in until the mixture resembles breadcrumbs. Stir in the sugar and grated root ginger. Set aside.

3. Put the evaporated milk and treacle or molasses in a saucepan and heat gently until just warm, stirring. Pour the treacle mixture into the flour mixture, add the eggs and stir together until well mixed.

4. Pour the mixture evenly into the prepared tin. Bake in the oven for about 50 minutes, or until a skewer inserted into the centre comes out clean. Leave to cool slightly in the tin, then turn out onto a wire rack and leave to cool completely. Serve in slices.

DEVONSHIRE HONEY Cake

This cake has a deep honey flavour complemented by the addition of orange zest. It is ideal for lunchboxes and picnics.

MAKES: 12–16 SLICES

225g unsalted butter
250g clear honey
100g light muscovado sugar
3 eggs, beaten
Finely grated zest of 1 orange
300g self-raising flour
80g pine nuts

CAKE TIP
For a change try using lemon zest instead of the orange and use slivered almonds in place of the pine nuts.

1. Preheat the oven to 170°C/325°F/Gas mark 3. Grease and base line a deep 20cm round cake tin.

2. Put the butter, honey and sugar in a saucepan and heat gently, stirring, until the butter has melted. Increase the heat and bring to the boil, then boil for 1 minute. Remove the pan from the heat and set aside to cool.

3. Beat the eggs and orange zest into the honey mixture. Sift the flour into a bowl and gradually beat in the honey mixture until smooth and well mixed. Pour the mixture evenly into the prepared tin and sprinkle the top with the pine nuts.

4. Bake in the oven for about 50–60 minutes, or until firm to the touch. Cool in the tin for 5–10 minutes, then turn out onto a wire rack and leave to cool completely. Serve in slices.

LADY BALTIMORE
Sponge Cake

MAKES: 12 SLICES

250g unsalted butter, softened
250g caster sugar
1 teaspoon vanilla extract
300g plain flour
1 tablespoon baking powder
¼ teaspoon salt
250ml milk
6 egg whites

FOR THE ICING

400g caster sugar
2 tablespoons golden syrup
4 egg whites
Pinch of cream of tartar
75g raisins
50g pecans, chopped
75g glacé cherries, chopped
1 teaspoon vanilla extract

1. Preheat the oven to 180°C/350°F/Gas mark 4. Grease and flour two 23cm round sandwich cake tins.

2. For the cake, cream the butter, 200g of the sugar and the vanilla extract together in a bowl until pale and fluffy. Sift the flour, baking powder and salt into a separate bowl. Fold the flour mixture and milk alternately into the creamed mixture.

3. In a separate bowl, whisk the egg whites until soft peaks form, then add the remaining 50g sugar and whisk until the mixture is stiff and glossy. Add one-third of the whisked egg whites to the cake mixture to lighten it, then gently fold in the rest. Pour the mixture into the prepared tins, dividing evenly.

4. Bake in the oven for 25–30 minutes, or until the cakes are golden and just firm to the touch. Turn out onto a wire rack and leave to cool.

5. Make the icing. Put the sugar in a medium, heavy-based saucepan with the golden syrup and 6 tablespoons of water. Stir to dissolve the sugar over a medium heat. Cook the sugar to medium ball stage, 118°C/245°F, without stirring. Meanwhile, whisk the egg whites and cream of tartar together in a bowl. When the sugar syrup has reached the correct temperature, pour it steadily into the egg whites, whisking continuously. Continue to whisk for 5 minutes, or until the icing is thick and creamy.

6. Stir the fruit, nuts and vanilla extract into the cooled icing and use to sandwich the cakes together. Spread over the top and sides and serve in slices.

ITALIAN RICOTTA
Cheesecake

Ricotta cheese makes a delicious light cheesecake. This is ideal served with fresh fruit for a tempting dessert.

MAKES: 10–12 SLICES

675g ricotta cheese
225g mascarpone cheese
150g caster sugar
2 tablespoons cornflour
4 eggs, beaten
2 teaspoons vanilla extract
$\frac{1}{4}$ teaspoon ground cinnamon
2 teaspoons finely grated lemon zest
Pinch of salt

1. Preheat the oven to 150°C/300°F/Gas mark 2. Grease a 23cm springform tin fitted with a flat base.

2. Beat the ricotta and mascarpone cheeses together in a large bowl until smooth, then stir in the sugar and cornflour, mixing well.

3. Gradually add the eggs, beating well to combine. Stir in the vanilla extract, cinnamon, lemon zest and salt, then pour the mixture evenly into the prepared tin. Bake in the oven for 50–60 minutes, or until the cheesecake is just firm to the touch.

4. Remove the cheesecake from the oven and leave to cool in the tin to room temperature, then cover with foil and refrigerate until ready to serve. Remove the cheesecake from the tin, place on a serving plate and serve in slices.

CHOCOLATE MARBLE Cake

This is an impressive cake to serve to friends or family. You can also cover the cake with chocolate icing if you like (see page 22 for Mississippi Mud Cake icing).

MAKES: 6–8 SLICES

175g self-raising flour
2 teaspoons baking powder
Pinch of salt
75g unsalted butter, softened
200g caster sugar
2 eggs, beaten
125ml milk
1 teaspoon vanilla extract
75g dark bitter chocolate, melted
175g icing sugar
4 tablespoons unsweetened cocoa
   powder

1. Preheat the oven to 180°C/350°F/Gas mark 4. Grease and base line a 20cm Angel cake tin.

2. Sift the flour, baking powder and salt into a bowl and set aside. Cream the butter and caster sugar together in a separate bowl, then gradually add the beaten eggs, a little at a time. Fold the flour and milk alternately into the creamed mixture, then stir in the vanilla extract.

3. Pour half the mixture into a separate bowl and stir in the melted chocolate. Spoon the batters alternately into the prepared tin, then draw a knife through the mixture to create a swirled marble effect.

4. Bake in the oven for 35–40 minutes, or until the cake is firm to the touch and a skewer inserted into the centre comes out clean. Cool the cake in the tin for 5 minutes, then turn out onto a wire rack and leave to cool completely.

5. Sift the icing sugar and cocoa powder into a bowl, then stir in enough warm water, mixing to form a thick pouring consistency. Spread or drizzle the icing evenly over the cake. Serve in slices.

APPLE CRUMB Cake

A great balance of flavours and textures creates this fantastic cake,
which is ideal for sharing with friends.

MAKES: 6–8 SLICES

140g unsalted butter
450g cooking apples, peeled, cored
   and chopped
½ teaspoon freshly grated nutmeg
1 teaspoon ground cinnamon
225g plain flour
150g caster sugar
2 eggs, beaten
3 tablespoons soured cream
1 teaspoon vanilla extract
½ teaspoon baking powder
¼ teaspoon bicarbonate of soda
Pinch of salt

CAKE TIP
*Serve this cake as a
pudding with vanilla
ice cream or a
creamy custard.*

1. Preheat the oven to 180°C/350°F/Gas mark 4. Grease and base line a deep 20cm round cake tin.

2. Melt 25g of the butter in a small saucepan. Add the apples, sprinkle in the nutmeg and half the cinnamon and stir to coat the apples in the butter. Place a disk of non-stick baking paper on top of the apples, reduce the heat and cook gently, stirring occasionally, for 5–10 minutes, or until the apples are tender. Remove the pan from the heat.

3. In a bowl, lightly rub 25g of the flour, 25g of the remaining butter and 25g of the sugar together, until the mixture forms large clumps. Set this crumb topping aside.

4. In a separate bowl, cream the remaining butter and sugar together, then gradually beat in the eggs. Beat in the soured cream and vanilla extract.

5. Sift the remaining flour and cinnamon, the baking powder, bicarbonate of soda and salt into the creamed mixture and fold in gently.

6. Stir in the warm apples, then spoon the mixture into the prepared tin and level the surface. Sprinkle over the reserved crumb topping. Bake in the oven for 40–45 minutes, or until a skewer inserted into the centre comes out clean. Turn out onto a wire rack and leave to cool. Serve in slices.

GOOSEBERRY & ELDERFLOWER Cake

A lovely moist cake that can also be served warm as a dessert. For a change, try using cooked plums, apples or rhubarb instead of gooseberries.

MAKES: 8–10 SLICES

280g self-raising flour
1 teaspoon baking powder
100g caster sugar
125g soft light brown sugar
125g unsalted butter, melted
2 eggs, beaten
350g cooked unsweetened
   gooseberries
2 tablespoons elderflower cordial
FOR THE ICING
125g icing sugar, sifted
3–5 teaspoons elderflower cordial

1. Preheat the oven to 180°C/350°F/Gas mark 4. Grease and base line a 23cm springform tin fitted with a flat base.

2. For the cake, mix the flour, baking powder and sugars together in a bowl. Add the melted butter and eggs and mix well. Stir in the gooseberries and elderflower cordial until well combined. Spoon the mixture into the prepared tin and level the surface.

3. Bake in the oven for about 45 minutes, or until a skewer inserted into the centre comes out clean. Cool in the tin for 5 minutes, then turn out onto a wire rack and leave to cool completely.

4. When the cake is cold, make the icing. Put the icing sugar in a bowl and stir in just enough elderflower cordial to make a thick pouring consistency. Using a teaspoon, drizzle the icing randomly and decoratively over the top of the cake. Serve in slices.

STRAWBERRY Shortcake

This classic summer recipe is sure to be a family favourite.

MAKES: 8 SLICES

400g self-raising flour
1½ tablespoons baking powder
¼ teaspoon salt
75g chilled unsalted butter, cut into
 small pieces
100g caster sugar
250ml buttermilk, plus extra for
 brushing
Jam (coarse) sugar, for sprinkling

FOR THE FILLING
185ml whipping cream
2 tablespoons icing sugar
½ teaspoon vanilla extract
450g strawberries, halved

1. Preheat the oven to 190°C/375°F/Gas mark 5. Grease and flour a baking sheet. Sift the flour, baking powder and salt into a bowl. Rub in the butter until the mixture resembles fine breadcrumbs.

2. Combine 65g of the caster sugar and the buttermilk in a bowl, then add this to the flour mixture. Mix to form a smooth dough, but do not overwork at this stage. Turn the dough onto a lightly floured surface and divide into two balls, one slightly larger than the other. Roll out each ball of dough to form a round about 2cm thick.

3. Place the dough rounds on the prepared baking sheet. Brush off any excess flour. Brush the tops with buttermilk and sprinkle with jam sugar. Bake in the oven for 20–25 minutes, or until golden. Transfer to a wire rack and leave to cool completely.

4. For the filling, whip the cream in a bowl until soft peaks form, then whisk in the icing sugar and vanilla extract, mixing well. Set aside.

5. Put the strawberries in a saucepan with 2 tablespoons of water and the remaining 35g of caster sugar and heat gently for 2–3 minutes to soften the fruit. Remove the pan from the heat.

6. Spoon the whipped cream onto the larger of the cooled shortcake rounds and spoon over the warm strawberries and juice. Top with the second shortcake round and serve immediately.

PLAITED FRUIT Loaf

This is an unusual and beautiful loaf. Vary the fruit and alcohol according to taste – substitute all vine fruits, for example, or use brandy instead of rum.

MAKES: 6-8 SLICES

175g mixed dried fruit, e.g. pineapple, raisins, sultanas, mixed peel, glacé cherries, roughly chopped
4 tablespoons rum
225g strong plain white flour
$\frac{1}{4}$ teaspoon salt
$1\frac{1}{2}$ teaspoons easy-blend dried yeast
2 tablespoons soft light brown sugar
100ml warmed milk
1 egg, beaten
50g ready-made marzipan, grated
6 tablespoons apricot jam
15g unsalted butter
1 tablespoon caster sugar
1 tablespoon clear honey

1. Put the mixed dried fruit in a bowl and stir in the rum. Cover and leave to soak overnight.

2. Combine the flour, salt, yeast and brown sugar in a bowl. Make a well in the centre and add the milk and egg. Mix to a soft dough, then knead for about 10 minutes, or until smooth. Shape into a ball and put into a clean oiled bowl. Cover and leave to rise in a warm place for about 1 hour, or until doubled in size.

3. Meanwhile, mix the soaked fruit, marzipan and apricot jam together. Preheat the oven to 200°C/400°F/Gas mark 6. Grease a baking sheet. Knead the dough again briefly for about 1 minute on a lightly floured surface, then roll out to form a 30 x 35cm rectangle. Trim to a neat shape.

4. Spread the fruit mixture in a 7.5cm strip down the centre of the rectangle leaving a margin of 5cm at each end. Make diagonal cuts, each about 2cm wide in the dough down either side of the filling.

5. Fold the strips of dough up over the filling, overlapping alternate strips. Tuck in the two ends. Transfer to the prepared baking sheet. Cover with oiled cling film and leave to rise for 20 minutes.

6. Meanwhile, melt the butter, caster sugar and honey together in a small saucepan, then brush this mixture evenly over the plaited loaf. Bake in the oven for 20–25 minutes, or until golden. Transfer to a wire rack to cool. Serve in slices.

CARAMEL PECAN Loaf

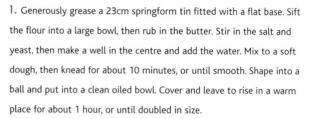

MAKES: 8–10 SLICES

450g strong plain white flour
15g unsalted butter
2 teaspoons salt
1½ teaspoons easy-blend dried yeast
300ml warmed water

FOR THE FILLING & TOPPING
175g unsalted butter
175g soft light brown sugar
100g pecans, roughly chopped
2 tablespoons double cream

1. Generously grease a 23cm springform tin fitted with a flat base. Sift the flour into a large bowl, then rub in the butter. Stir in the salt and yeast, then make a well in the centre and add the water. Mix to a soft dough, then knead for about 10 minutes, or until smooth. Shape into a ball and put into a clean oiled bowl. Cover and leave to rise in a warm place for about 1 hour, or until doubled in size.

2. Knead the dough again briefly for about 1 minute on a lightly floured surface, then pat out to form a 25 x 35cm rectangle. Trim to a neat shape. Cover and leave to rest for 10 minutes. Preheat the oven to 200°C/400°F/Gas mark 6.

3. Meanwhile, cream 100g of the butter and 100g of the sugar together in a bowl until smooth. Stir in most of the pecans. Spread the mixture evenly over the dough, leaving a 2.5cm margin around the edges. Starting from a long side, roll up the dough tightly and cut into 5cm slices. Arrange the slices in the prepared tin, cut-side up. Cover and leave to rise for about 30 minutes, or until the dough has risen to the top of the tin.

4. Bake the loaf in the oven for 30–40 minutes, or until risen and golden, covering the top with foil if it begins to over-brown.

5. Meanwhile, melt the remaining butter and sugar together in a saucepan over a low heat. Add the cream and bring to the boil. Simmer for 3–4 minutes, then add the remaining pecans and cook for 1 minute. Remove from the heat.

6. Remove the loaf from the oven and immediately spread the pecan mixture evenly over the top. Cool in the tin, then turn out and serve in slices.

ALMOND MACAROON Cake

A simple fruit cake with an unusual almond macaroon topping. This cake improves if kept wrapped in foil for a couple of days before cutting.

MAKES: 10 SLICES

175g unsalted butter, softened
175g caster sugar
3 eggs, beaten
1 egg yolk
175g plain flour
1 teaspoon almond extract
125g chopped mixed peel
125g sultanas
125g raisins
125g natural-colour glacé cherries, halved

FOR THE TOPPING
1 egg white
125g caster sugar
80g ground almonds
½ teaspoon almond extract
2–3 tablespoons flaked almonds

1. Preheat the oven to 170°C/325°F/Gas mark 3. Grease the base and sides of a deep 20cm round cake tin and double-line with non-stick baking paper.

2. For the cake, beat the butter and sugar together in a bowl until light and fluffy. Gradually beat in the eggs and egg yolk, adding a little flour if the mixture begins to curdle.

3. Fold in the remaining flour and the almond extract. Add the mixed peel, sultanas, raisins and glacé cherries, mixing well. Turn the mixture into the prepared tin and level the surface. Set aside.

4. For the topping, whisk the egg white in a bowl until light and fluffy but not stiff. Whisk in the sugar, then fold in the ground almonds and almond extract. Spread this almond mixture evenly over the top of the cake mixture in the tin. Sprinkle with the flaked almonds.

5. Place in the oven and put a baking sheet on top of the cake tin to cover it completely. Bake for 1¼–1½ hours, or until a skewer inserted into the centre comes out clean. Remove the cake from the oven and remove the baking sheet. Leave the cake to cool in the tin, then carefully turn out and serve in slices.

FRUIT Gingerbread

Everyone will enjoy this afternoon treat – it's really a cross
between a cake and a teabread, and it is delicious served
sliced with butter.

MAKES: 6–8 SQUARES

400g plain flour
1 teaspoon baking powder
1 tablespoon ground ginger
1 teaspoon ground cinnamon
225g unsalted butter
125g molasses or black treacle
175g soft light brown sugar
3 eggs, beaten
75g dried cherries, halved
115g stoned dried dates, chopped
50g preserved stem ginger, drained
   and chopped
90g sultanas

1. Preheat the oven to 150°C/300°F/Gas mark 2. Grease and base line a
deep 20cm square cake tin.

2. Mix the flour, baking powder, ground ginger and cinnamon in a large
bowl. Set aside. Place the butter in a saucepan with the molasses or black
treacle and sugar and stir over a low heat until melted. Pour into the flour
mixture and mix well. Beat in the eggs until smooth, then stir in the dried
cherries, dates, stem ginger and sultanas, mixing well.

3. Pour the mixture evenly into the prepared tin. Bake in the oven for
1–1¼ hours, or until a skewer inserted into the centre comes out clean.
Cool in the tin for 10 minutes,
then turn out onto a wire
rack and leave to cool
completely. Serve in
slices or squares.

APPLE & RASPBERRY Cake

This delicious moist sponge is ideal for lunchboxes or picnics.

MAKES: 6–8 SQUARES

150g unsalted butter, chopped
200g caster sugar
2 eggs, lightly beaten
1 teaspoon vanilla essence
185g self-raising flour, sifted
185g vanilla-flavoured yoghurt
1 large apple, peeled, cored and grated
100g raspberries
Sifted icing sugar, for dusting

1. Preheat the oven to 180°C/350°F/Gas mark 4. Grease and base line a 20cm round cake tin.

2. Beat the butter and sugar together in a bowl until pale and fluffy. Gradually add the eggs, beating well after each addition. Stir in the vanilla essence. Add the flour, then the yoghurt, grated apple and raspberries and mix until smooth.

3. Spoon the mixture into the prepared tin and level the surface. Bake in the oven for 1 hour, or until golden and the centre of the cake springs back when lightly pressed.

4. Leave in the tin for 30 minutes before turning out onto a wire rack to cool completely. Dust with icing sugar before serving.

CAKE TIP
Instead of apples and raspberries try using pear and blueberries or blackberries as an alternative.

RICH BUTTER Cake

Use the best-quality ingredients you can for this loaf cake
and you'll taste the difference.

MAKES: 10–12 SLICES

250g self-raising flour
1 teaspoon baking powder
250g unsalted butter, softened
200g caster sugar
3 eggs, beaten
3 tablespoons semi-skimmed milk
1 teaspoon vanilla extract

CAKE TIP
*For a crunchy top,
scatter roughly
crushed sugar cubes on
top of the cake
before baking.*

1. Preheat the oven to 180°C/350°F/Gas mark 4. Grease and base line a 900g loaf tin.

2. Sift the flour and baking powder into a bowl. Set aside. Cream the butter and sugar together in a separate bowl and beat for 4–5 minutes, or until pale and fluffy. Gradually beat in the eggs, milk and vanilla extract, then fold in the flour until well mixed. Spoon the mixture into the prepared tin and level the surface.

3. Bake in the oven for 50–55 minutes, or until firm to the touch and a skewer inserted into the centre comes out clean. Cool in the tin for 10 minutes, then turn out onto a wire rack and leave to cool completely. Serve in slices.

TROPICAL FRUIT Cake

To make this cake more decorative, reserve some of the chopped tropical fruit and scatter it over the top of the cake mixture just before baking.

MAKES: 8–10 SLICES

150g unsalted butter, softened
150g caster sugar
2 eggs, beaten
150g self-raising flour
2 tablespoons coconut cream
250g ready-to-eat mixed dried
   tropical fruit, chopped
50g macadamia nuts, chopped

1. Preheat the oven to 180°C/350°F/Gas mark 4. Grease and base line a 450g loaf tin.

2. Beat the butter and sugar together in a bowl until light and fluffy. Gradually add the eggs, beating well after each addition. Fold in the flour, then stir in the coconut cream.

3. Stir in the tropical fruit and macadamia nuts. Spoon the mixture into the prepared tin and level the surface.

4. Bake in the oven for about 50 minutes, or until a skewer inserted into the centre comes out clean. Cool in the tin for 5–10 minutes, then turn out onto a wire rack and leave to cool completely. Serve in slices.

CHOCOLATE REFRIGERATOR Cake

Refrigerator cakes are always a great favourite with adults and kids alike. This one is simple and quick to make and you can substitute any preferred fruits, if you like.

MAKES: 12–14 SLICES

450g dark bitter chocolate, broken
   into squares
250g unsalted butter
350g shortbread biscuits or digestive
   biscuits, roughly chopped
200g pecans, chopped
150g raisins
150g red glacé cherries, halved
50g mini marshmallows

1. Grease and line a 900g loaf tin with a double layer of cling film.

2. Melt the chocolate and butter together in a large heat-proof mixing bowl set over a pan of gently simmering water. Remove the bowl from the heat. Add all the remaining ingredients and stir together until well mixed.

3. Spoon the mixture into the prepared tin and level the surface. Cover and refrigerate for 2–3 hours, or until firm enough to turn out. Serve in slices.

CAKE TIP
You can substitute ginger biscuits or any other of your favourite biscuits for those used in this recipe if you wish.

AFTERNOON
TEA

CHERRY LOAF Cake

Here is a loaf cake that is quick and simple to make – the perfect
cake to bake in a hurry if unexpected guests arrive for a cup of tea.

MAKES: 10–12 SLICES

225g plain flour
1 teaspoon baking powder
250g unsalted butter, softened
200g caster sugar
3 eggs, beaten
3 tablespoons semi-skimmed milk
1 teaspoon vanilla extract
50g ground almonds
150g glacé cherries, cut in half

1. Preheat the oven to 180°C/350°F/Gas mark 4. Grease and base line
a 900g loaf tin.

2. Sift the flour and baking powder into a bowl. In a separate bowl,
cream the butter and sugar together until pale and fluffy. Gradually beat
in the eggs, milk and vanilla extract until well combined. Fold in the flour,
ground almonds and glacé cherries.

3. Spoon the mixture into the prepared tin and level the surface.
Bake in the oven for 50–55 minutes, or until firm to the touch and a
skewer inserted into the centre comes out clean. Cool in the tin for 10
minutes, then turn out onto a wire rack and leave to cool completely.
Serve in slices.

CAKE TIP
*To stop glacé
cherries sinking, wash
and pat them dry
before using.*

CINNAMON SWIRL Bread

MAKES: 10–12 SLICES

750g strong plain white flour
125g granulated sugar
1 teaspoon salt
2 teaspoons fast-action dried yeast
125g unsalted butter
400ml milk
2 eggs, beaten
4 heaped tablespoons soft light
  brown sugar
2 teaspoons ground cinnamon
Sifted icing sugar, to decorate

1. Place the flour, granulated sugar and salt in a large bowl, then stir in the yeast. Make a well in the centre of the mixture.

2. Melt the butter in a saucepan. Add the milk to the melted butter and heat until it is just warm or hand hot. Pour the mixture into the well in the flour, add the eggs and mix together with a wooden spoon until you have a smooth dough.

3. Cover the dough and leave to rise in a warm place for 45–60 minutes, or until it has doubled in size. Meanwhile, mix the brown sugar with the cinnamon and set aside. Grease a 2.4 litre Kugelhopf mould.

4. Beat the dough with a wooden spoon to knock it back. With well-floured hands, divide the dough into four equal pieces.

5. Place a piece of dough in the prepared mould and stretch it around the base until it is covered. Sprinkle over a quarter of the cinnamon sugar mixture. Take a second piece of dough and stretch it over the first one. Sprinkle with cinnamon sugar. Repeat twice more. Leave to rise for 15 minutes. Meanwhile preheat the oven to 220°C/425°F/Gas mark 7.

6. Bake the loaf in the oven for 20 minutes, then reduce the oven temperature to 190°C/375°F/Gas mark 5 and bake for a further 5–10 minutes, or until the bread is risen and sounds hollow when tapped underneath. Turn out onto a wire rack and leave to cool. Dredge the bread with sifted icing sugar and serve in slices.

SWISS ROLL with
Lemon Cream

MAKES: 6–8 SLICES

4 large eggs
100g caster sugar, plus extra for
  dusting
100g plain flour
Sifted icing sugar and finely grated
  lemon zest, to decorate

FOR THE FILLING
250g mascarpone cheese
Finely grated zest and juice of ½
  lemon
2 tablespoons freshly squeezed
  orange juice
4 tablespoons icing sugar

1. Preheat the oven to 220°C/425°F/Gas mark 7. Grease and line a
23 x 33cm Swiss roll tin.

2. For the sponge, using a hand-held electric mixer, whisk the eggs and
sugar together in a large bowl until the mixture is pale, creamy and thick
enough to leave a trail on the surface when the whisk is lifted.

3. Sift and fold in the flour in three batches. Pour the mixture into the
prepared tin, tilting the tin backwards and forwards to spread evenly. Bake
in the oven for about 10 minutes, or until risen and golden and the cake
springs back when lightly pressed.

4. While the cake is cooking, lay a sheet of greaseproof paper on a work
surface and sprinkle liberally with caster sugar.

5. Quickly turn the hot cake out onto the sugar-dusted paper and
remove the lining paper. Trim off the crusty edges, score a cut 1cm in
from one of the shorter ends, then roll up the cake from the scored short
end with the paper inside. Place on a wire rack and leave to cool.

6. For the filling, put all the filling ingredients in a bowl and beat
together until smooth and well mixed. Carefully unroll the cake, remove
the paper and spread the filling mixture evenly over the cake. Re-roll the
cake. To decorate, dredge the cake with sifted icing sugar and sprinkle
with lemon zest. Serve in slices.

CARIBBEAN BANANA Bread

A great way to use up over-ripe bananas that no one wants to eat —
they are transformed into a delicious, moist and spicy cake.

MAKES: 6–8 SLICES

2 bananas, peeled
2 tablespoons clear honey
200g self-raising flour
½ teaspoon baking powder
1 teaspoon freshly grated nutmeg
150g unsalted butter, softened
175g soft light brown sugar
2 eggs, beaten
50g pecans, finely chopped

1. Preheat the oven to 180°C/350°F/Gas mark 4. Grease and base line a 450g loaf tin.

2. Mash the bananas in a bowl with the honey. Sift the flour, baking powder and nutmeg into a separate bowl.

3. Cream the butter and sugar together in a large mixing bowl until pale and fluffy, then gradually add the eggs, beating well after each addition.

4. Fold in the bananas and the flour mixture together with the pecans. Spoon the mixture into the prepared tin and level the surface. Bake in the oven for 50–60 minutes, or until risen and golden and a skewer inserted into the centre comes out clean.

5. Cool in the tin for 10 minutes, then turn out onto a wire rack and leave to cool completely. Serve in slices.

ORANGE & ALMOND
Sponge Cake

This moist iced sponge cake is a great accompaniment to morning coffee or afternoon tea and it is special enough for dessert, too.

MAKES: 6–8 SLICES

175g unsalted butter
175g caster sugar
3 eggs, beaten
150g self-raising flour
50g ground almonds
Few drops of almond extract
Toasted flaked almonds and thinly
    pared orange zest, to decorate

FOR THE ICING
280g cream cheese or full-fat
    soft cheese
2 tablespoons freshly squeezed
    orange juice
2 teaspoons finely grated orange zest
100g icing sugar, sifted

1. Preheat the oven to 190°C/375°F/Gas mark 5. Grease and base line two 20cm round sandwich cake tins.

2. For the cake, beat the butter and sugar together in a bowl until pale and fluffy. Gradually add the eggs, beating well after each addition. Sift the flour over the creamed mixture, then gently fold in with the ground almonds and almond extract until well combined.

3. Spoon the mixture into the prepared tins, dividing it evenly, then level the surface. Bake in the oven for 20–25 minutes, or until risen and golden and the centres of the cakes spring back when lightly pressed. Turn out onto a wire rack and leave to cool.

4. Meanwhile, make the icing. Beat the cream cheese or soft cheese in a bowl to soften. Add the orange juice, orange zest and icing sugar and beat together until smooth and creamy.

5. Sandwich the two cakes together with a little icing, then spread the remaining icing over the top of the cake. Scatter with toasted, flaked almonds and orange zest to decorate. Serve in slices.

AMERICAN WHISKED
Sponge Cake

This traditional American light-as-a-feather sponge cake recipe is flavoured
with vanilla and is perfect served with fruit and cream for afternoon tea.

MAKES: 6–8 SLICES

3 large eggs, separated
100g caster sugar
1 teaspoon vanilla extract
¼ teaspoon cream of tartar
100g plain flour, sifted
Pinch of salt
300ml double cream
100g fresh strawberries
Sifted icing sugar, for dusting

1. Preheat the oven to 180°C/350°F/Gas mark 4. Grease and base line
two 20cm round sandwich cake tins.

2. Using a hand-held electric mixer, whisk the egg yolks and 50g of the
caster sugar together in a bowl until the mixture is pale and creamy.
Whisk in the vanilla extract. Set aside.

3. In a separate bowl, whisk the egg whites and cream of tartar together
until they are stiff. Gradually whisk in the remaining caster sugar until the
mixture is stiff and glossy. Sift the flour and salt over the egg yolk
mixture and fold in with a quarter of the whisked egg whites. Fold in the
remaining whisked egg whites.

4. Pour the mixture into the prepared tins, dividing it evenly. Bake in the
oven for about 30 minutes, or until golden and the tops spring back when
lightly pressed. Turn out onto a wire rack and leave to cool.

5. Whip the cream in a bowl to form soft peaks. Chop all but 1–2
strawberries. Sandwich the cakes together with the whipped cream and
chopped strawberries. Dust the top of the cake with sifted icing sugar and
decorate with small whole or halved strawberries.

SIMPLE ALMOND Cake

This light and simple cake packed with ground almonds is delicious served
with fresh fruit and whipped cream for a filling afternoon-tea treat.

MAKES: 8–10 SLICES

2 tablespoons plain flour, sifted
250g ground almonds
7 large egg whites
200g caster sugar
2 tablespoons orange-flavoured
   liqueur
150ml whipping cream, whipped to
   form soft peaks
175g strawberries, sliced
Sifted icing sugar, for dusting

1. Preheat the oven to 180°C/350°F/Gas mark 4. Grease and line a
23cm springform tin fitted with a flat base.

2. Sift the flour into a bowl, then stir in the ground almonds. Set aside.
Whisk the egg whites in a separate bowl until stiff. Gradually whisk in the
200g caster sugar, until the mixture is stiff and glossy.

3. Gently fold the flour and almond mixture into the whisked egg whites.
Spoon the mixture into the prepared tin and level the surface. Bake in the
oven for 25–30 minutes, or until golden and spongy to the touch.

4. Remove the cake from the oven and leave to cool completely in the
tin, then turn out onto a board. Slice the cake in half horizontally, then
drizzle the orange liqueur over each half. Spread one half of the cake, cut-
side up, with the whipped cream and top with the sliced strawberries. Top
with the second cake half, cut-side down, and dust with sifted icing sugar.
Serve in slices.

CAKE TIP
*To prevent the cream
becoming over-whipped,
slightly under-whip the cream
and then finish with a hand
whisk or a very low speed on
an electric mixer.*

ANGEL
FOOD Cake

A truly magnificent feat in the art of cake-making, this
impressive cake is held together almost by air.

MAKES: 8–10 SLICES

50g plain flour
1 tablespoon cornflour
200g caster sugar
7 egg whites
³/₄ teaspoon cream of tartar
Pinch of salt
1¹/₂ teaspoons vanilla extract
2 tablespoons toasted chopped
    pistachio nuts, to decorate

FOR THE ICING
2 egg whites
350g caster sugar
¹/₄ teaspoon cream of tartar

1. Preheat the oven to 180°C/350°F/Gas mark 4. Grease and line a
23cm springform tin fitted with a tube base.

2. For the cake, sift the flour and cornflour into a bowl. Add 65g of the
sugar and sift together twice.

3. In a separate large bowl, whisk the egg whites until foamy. Add the
cream of tartar and salt and whisk until stiff. Whisk the remaining sugar
into the egg whites until the mixture is stiff and glossy. Whisk in the
vanilla extract.

4. Carefully fold in the flour mixture, then spoon the batter into the
prepared tin and level the surface. Bake in the oven for 45–50 minutes, or
until pale golden and spongy to the touch. Place the cake tin on a wire
rack and leave to cool in the tin.

5. To make the icing, put all the icing ingredients in a heat-proof bowl,
add 4 tablespoons of water and set the bowl over a pan of hot water.
Using a hand-held electric mixer, whisk the mixture for 10–12 minutes,
or until thick.

6. Run a knife around the inside edge of the tin and remove the cold
cake. Spread the icing evenly over the top and sides of the cake and finish
with a sprinkling of toasted chopped pistachio nuts.

SPICED APPLE, CRANBERRY & CIDER Cake

This is an attractive cake, which is very fruity and not overly sweet. As it contains fresh fruit it is best eaten within a couple of days of making, or keep it refrigerated.

MAKES: 6–8 SLICES

3 medium red-skinned eating apples
100g dried sweetened cranberries
200ml dry cider
350g self-raising flour
2 teaspoons ground cinnamon
175g light muscovado sugar
175g unsalted butter, melted
3 eggs, beaten

FOR THE TOPPING

1 medium red-skinned eating apple,
   thinly sliced and pips removed
3 tablespoons apricot jam, warmed

1. For the cake, peel and core the apples, then chop them roughly. Put the apples, cranberries and cider in a saucepan and bring to the boil, then simmer very gently for 5 minutes. Remove the pan from the heat and set aside to cool completely.

2. Preheat the oven to 180°C/350°F/Gas mark 4. Grease and base line a 20cm springform tin fitted with a flat base.

3. Sift the flour and cinnamon into a bowl and stir in the sugar. Add the melted butter, eggs and apple and cider mixture. Stir until just combined, then spoon into the prepared tin and level the surface. For the topping, arrange the apple slices evenly over the top of the cake mixture.

4. Bake in the oven for 50–60 minutes, or until a skewer inserted into the centre comes out clean. Leave to cool in the tin for 5 minutes, then turn out onto a wire rack.

5. Brush the apricot jam over the top of the cake while it is still warm. Leave to cool completely, then serve in slices.

GOLDEN BUTTERCREAM Cake

Rich and buttery, this cake is an anytime cake. Eat and enjoy!

MAKES: 6–8 SLICES

250g sponge (premium self-raising)
    flour
2 teaspoons baking powder
Pinch of salt
225g unsalted butter, softened
250g caster sugar
4 eggs, beaten
1 teaspoon vanilla extract
FOR THE ICING
125g unsalted butter, softened
1 teaspoon vanilla extract
200g icing sugar, sifted
3–4 drops of yellow food colouring

1. Preheat the oven to 180°C/350°F/Gas mark 4. Grease and base line two 20cm round sandwich cake tins.

2. For the cake, sift the flour, baking powder and salt into a bowl. In a separate bowl, beat the butter until pale and fluffy. Add the sugar and beat for a further 2 minutes. Gradually add the eggs, beating well after each addition. Add the vanilla extract, then fold in the flour mixture.

3. Spoon the mixture into the prepared tins, dividing it evenly, and level the surface. Bake in the oven for 30–35 minutes, or until risen, golden and firm to the touch. Turn out onto a wire rack and leave to cool.

4. For the icing, beat the butter and vanilla extract together in a bowl until pale and fluffy, then stir in the icing sugar. Add the yellow food colouring and beat to mix well. Sandwich the two cakes together with some icing, then spread the remaining icing over the top of the cake. Serve in slices.

FRUIT TEA Loaf

This recipe is incredibly easy to make, and the cake is a great standby in case family or friends visit. It's delicious served in slices spread with butter.

MAKES: 8–10 SLICES

300g mixed dried fruit, such as sultanas, currants, raisins and glacé cherries
125g soft light brown sugar
125g unsalted butter
200ml brewed tea
2 teaspoons ground allspice
Finely grated zest of 1 orange
225g self-raising flour, sifted
1 tablespoon clear honey, warmed

CAKE TIP
For a scented flavour use a tea such as Earl or Lady Grey.

1. Place the mixed dried fruit, sugar, butter, tea and allspice in a saucepan. Cover and heat gently until the butter has melted, stirring occasionally. Bring to the boil and boil for 1 minute, then remove the pan from the heat. Add the orange zest, then set aside and leave overnight.

2. Preheat the oven to 180°C/350°F/Gas mark 4. Grease and base line a 450g loaf tin.

3. Fold the sifted flour into the fruit mixture. Spoon the mixture into the prepared tin and level the surface. Bake in the oven for 50–55 minutes, or until golden and a skewer inserted into the centre comes out clean.

4. Remove the cake from the oven, brush the top of the cake with warmed honey, then leave it to cool completely in the tin. Turn out and serve in slices spread with butter, if you like.

DATE & WALNUT Loaf

This is a lovely moist cake that slices well and
keeps for more than a week if wrapped in foil.

MAKES: 12–14 SLICES

125g unsalted butter
125g light muscovado sugar
50g golden syrup
150ml milk
2 large eggs, beaten
250g plain flour
1 level teaspoon bicarbonate of soda
1 teaspoon ground mixed spice
150g stoned dried dates, chopped
50g walnuts, chopped

FOR THE TOPPING
50g stoned dried dates, chopped
25g walnuts, chopped
1 tablespoon caster sugar
1 teaspoon ground cinnamon

1. Preheat the oven to 150°C/300°F/Gas mark 2. Grease and base line a
900g loaf tin.

2. For the cake, put the butter, sugar and golden syrup in a large
saucepan and heat gently, stirring. When the butter has melted, remove
the pan from the heat and set aside to cool for a few minutes.

3. Stir the milk and eggs into the syrup mixture. Sift the flour,
bicarbonate of soda and mixed spice into a bowl, then stir in the syrup
mixture. Mix to a smooth batter, then fold in the dates and walnuts.

4. Pour the mixture evenly into the prepared tin. Mix the topping
ingredients together and sprinkle thickly over the top of the cake.

5. Bake in the oven for 1–1¼ hours, or until a
skewer inserted into the centre
comes out clean. Cool in the tin
for 5 minutes, then turn out
onto a wire rack and leave to
cool completely. Serve in slices.

ORANGE CHIFFON Cake

Light and flavourful, this citrus cake is delicious served on its own or with some fruit for a tempting afternoon tea.

MAKES: 12–14 SLICES

225g sponge (premium self-raising) flour
2 teaspoons baking powder
Pinch of salt
300g caster sugar
125ml safflower or sunflower oil
3 eggs, separated
175ml unsweetened orange juice
2 tablespoons finely grated orange zest
1 teaspoon vanilla extract
Pinch of cream of tartar

1. Preheat the oven to 170°C/325°F/Gas mark 3. Grease a 25cm Bundt tin.

2. Combine the flour, baking powder, salt and sugar in a bowl. Make a well in the centre of the dry ingredients and add the oil, egg yolks, orange juice, orange zest and vanilla extract. Beat together for about 1 minute, or until smooth.

3. In a separate bowl, whisk the egg whites until they start to form soft peaks. Add the cream of tartar and whisk until stiff peaks form. Fold the whisked egg whites into the cake mixture using a balloon whisk.

4. Pour the mixture evenly into the prepared tin. Bake in the oven for 55 minutes, or until firm to the touch. Invert the cake onto a wire rack, but leave to cool in the tin. Run a knife around the inside edges of the tin and remove the cold cake. Serve in slices.

GERMAN CHOCOLATE Cake

A rich and buttery, nutty icing works well with this light chocolate sponge, which is ideal for sharing with friends for afternoon tea.

MAKES: 8–10 SLICES

115g dark bitter chocolate
175g unsalted butter
300g caster sugar
3 eggs, beaten
200g sponge (premium self-raising)
   flour
1 teaspoon bicarbonate of soda
Pinch of salt
250ml buttermilk

FOR THE FILLING
350ml evaporated milk
300g caster sugar
175g unsalted butter
4 egg yolks
2 teaspoons vanilla extract
200g sweetened flaked or desiccated
   coconut
150g pecans, chopped

1. Preheat the oven to 180°C/350°F/Gas mark 4. Grease and base line three 20cm round sandwich cake tins.

2. For the cake, melt the chocolate and butter in a large heat-proof bowl set over a pan of gently simmering water. Stir to melt the chocolate, then stir in the sugar. Remove from the heat, then using a hand-held electric mixer, gradually beat in the eggs using a low speed.

3. Beat in 50g of the flour, the bicarbonate of soda and salt. Add the remaining flour alternately with the buttermilk. Beat well for 1 minute to produce a smooth batter.

4. Divide the mixture between the prepared tins, dividing it evenly, then level the surface. Bake in the oven for 25–30 minutes, or until risen and just firm to the touch. Turn out onto a wire rack and leave to cool.

5. For the filling, pour the evaporated milk into a saucepan and add the sugar, butter, egg yolks and vanilla extract. Cook over a medium heat for 10–12 minutes, stirring continuously. The mixture will thicken and turn golden brown. Remove the pan from the heat, strain the mixture through a sieve, then stir in the coconut and pecans. Cool the mixture to room temperature before using it to sandwich together and cover the three sponge cakes. Serve in slices.

SIMPLE RAISIN FRUIT Cake

Ground allspice and vanilla extract flavour this sumptuous raisin cake – perfect served with morning coffee or afternoon tea.

MAKES: 12–14 SLICES

250g plain flour
1 teaspoon baking powder
225g unsalted butter, softened
200g caster sugar
3 eggs, beaten
3 tablespoons semi-skimmed milk
1 teaspoon vanilla extract
½ teaspoon ground allspice
200g raisins
Sifted icing sugar, to dust

1. Preheat the oven to 180°C/350°F/Gas mark 4. Grease and base line a 900g loaf tin.

2. Sift the flour and baking powder into a bowl. In a separate bowl, cream the butter and caster sugar together until pale and fluffy. Gradually beat in the eggs, milk and vanilla extract until well combined. Fold in the flour, allspice and raisins.

3. Spoon the mixture into the prepared tin and level the surface. Bake in the oven for 50–55 minutes, or until firm to the touch and a skewer inserted into the centre comes out clean.

4. Cool in the tin for 10 minutes, then turn out onto a wire rack and leave to cool completely. Dust lightly with icing sugar and serve in slices.

CAKE TIP
To make this cake even more delicious, soak the raisins overnight in the juice of 1 orange.

POUND CAKE
with Butter Syrup

Pound cake is a very old recipe originally using a pound of each ingredient –
butter, sugar, eggs and flour. This scaled-down version has a lovely butter glaze.

MAKES: 16–20 SLICES

300g unsalted butter, softened
300g caster sugar
2 teaspoons finely grated lemon zest
175g plain flour
175g potato flour
1½ teaspoons baking powder
6 eggs, beaten
2 tablespoons milk
FOR THE GLAZE
100g caster sugar
50g unsalted butter
1 teaspoon vanilla extract

1. Preheat the oven to 180°C/350°F/Gas mark 4. Prepare a 23cm Bundt
tin by brushing it twice with melted butter and dusting lightly with flour.

2. For the cake, beat the butter and sugar together in a bowl until pale
and fluffy. Stir in the lemon zest. In a separate bowl, sift together the
plain flour, potato flour and baking powder.

3. Gradually beat the eggs into the creamed mixture, adding a little of
the flour if the mixture begins to curdle. Fold in the remaining flour
mixture, then stir in the milk until well mixed. Spoon the mixture into the
prepared tin and level the surface.

4. Bake in the oven for 45–55 minutes, or until a skewer inserted into
the centre comes out clean. Remove the cake from the oven and ease it
away from the sides of the tin. Leave to cool in the tin for 10 minutes
before turning out onto a wire rack.

5. To make the glaze, put the sugar, butter and 4 tablespoons of water in
a saucepan and heat gently, stirring until the butter has melted. Simmer
gently for 3 minutes, then remove the pan from the heat and stir in the
vanilla extract. Pour the butter glaze evenly over the warm cake and leave
to cool completely. Serve in slices.

CHOCOLATE Layer Cake

MAKES: 10 SLICES

225g plain flour
1½ teaspoons bicarbonate of soda
½ teaspoon baking powder
1 teaspoon salt
350g caster sugar
2 teaspoons vanilla extract
300ml buttermilk
125g white vegetable margarine
3 eggs
75g plain chocolate, melted and
  cooled
Chocolate leaves or curls, to decorate
  (optional)
FOR THE FUDGE ICING
250ml double cream
450g good-quality plain or dark bitter
  chocolate, chopped
75g unsalted butter, at room
  temperature
1 tablespoon vanilla extract

CAKE TIP
*For a four-layer cake,
slice the two cakes in half
horizontally and ice between
each layer, ending with the last
layer of cake flat-side up, then
ice the top and sides of the
cake as above.*

1. Preheat the oven to 180°C/350°F/Gas mark 4. Grease and flour two 23cm round sandwich cake tins.

2. Sift the flour, bicarbonate of soda, baking powder and salt into a large mixing bowl. Add the sugar, vanilla extract, buttermilk, margarine, eggs and cooled melted chocolate. Using a hand-held electric mixer on low speed, begin to beat the mixture slowly until the ingredients are well blended, then increase the mixer speed to high and beat for 5 minutes, scraping down the sides of the bowl occasionally.

3. Spoon the mixture into the prepared tins, dividing it evenly, then level the surface. Bake in the oven for about 25 minutes, or until the tops of the cakes are set. A skewer inserted into the centre should come out with just one or two crumbs attached. Cool in the tins for 10 minutes, then turn out onto a wire rack and leave to cool completely.

4. To make the icing, pour the cream into a saucepan and bring to the boil over a medium-high heat. Remove the pan from the heat and add the chocolate, stirring until melted and smooth. Beat in the butter and vanilla extract until well combined. Chill in the refrigerator, stirring every 10–15 minutes, until the icing becomes quite thick and spreadable. Remove from the refrigerator and continue to stir occasionally until the icing is thick.

5. Place one cake, top-side up, on a plate and spread evenly with about a quarter of the chocolate icing. Place the second cake on top, flat-side up, then spread the top and sides of the cake with the remaining icing, making deep swirls with a palette knife or the back of a spoon. Decorate with chocolate leaves or curls, if using. Serve in slices.

CARROT & BRAZIL NUT Traybake

This is a very easy cake to make and it is equally good with or without the icing. It makes a healthy addition to a packed lunch.

MAKES: 18 SQUARES

300g self-raising flour
350g caster sugar
2 teaspoons baking powder
100g Brazil nuts, chopped
2 teaspoons ground cinnamon
1 teaspoon ground ginger
300ml sunflower oil
300g carrots, grated
4 eggs, beaten
1 teaspoon vanilla extract

FOR THE TOPPING
400g low-fat soft cheese
1 tablespoon clear honey
Brazil nuts, to decorate

1. Preheat the oven to 180°C/350°F/Gas mark 4. Grease and base line a 30 x 23cm cake tin.

2. For the cake, put the flour, sugar, baking powder, Brazil nuts, cinnamon and ground ginger in a large bowl. Add the sunflower oil, grated carrots, eggs and vanilla extract and beat together to mix well. Pour the mixture evenly into the prepared tin.

3. Bake in the oven for about 50 minutes, or until firm to the touch. Cool in the tin for 5–10 minutes, then turn out onto a wire rack and leave to cool completely.

4. For the topping, combine the soft cheese and honey in a bowl. Spread the topping mixture evenly over the top of the cake. Decorate with Brazil nuts and serve in slices or squares.

LEMON & GINGER Cake

This sharp-tasting, moist cake will keep well – if it lasts long enough!

MAKES: 12–14 SLICES

250g plain flour
1 teaspoon baking powder
250g unsalted butter, softened
200g caster sugar
3 eggs, beaten
3 tablespoons semi-skimmed milk
50g ground almonds
1 teaspoon ground ginger
2 tablespoons finely grated lemon
   zest
2 tablespoons finely shredded
   candied lemon peel

1. Preheat the oven to 180°C/350°F/Gas mark 4. Grease and base line a 900g loaf tin.

2. Sift the flour and baking powder into a bowl. In a separate bowl, cream the butter and sugar together until pale and fluffy. Gradually beat in the eggs and milk, then fold in the flour, ground almonds, ginger and lemon zest.

3. Spoon the mixture into the prepared tin and level the surface. Bake in the oven for 55–60 minutes, or until firm to the touch and a skewer inserted into the centre comes out clean.

4. Cool in the tin for 10 minutes, then turn out onto a wire rack and leave to cool completely. Spoon the candied lemon peel evenly over the top of the cake. Serve in slices.

CAKE TIP

To make your own candied peel, place pared strips of unwaxed lemon peel from 2 lemons in a small pan of water and bring to the boil. Drain and refresh under cold water. Repeat this process. Finely shred the peel, return it to the pan with enough water to cover and 100g caster sugar. Heat gently to dissolve the sugar, then bring to the boil and simmer until the syrup thickens. Remove the pan from the heat and cool slightly. Spoon the candied peel over the top of the cake to decorate.

COFFEE, MAPLE & PECAN SPONGE Cake

MAKES: 6–8 SLICES

75g plain flour
Pinch of salt
40g unsalted butter
3 large eggs
75g caster sugar
1 teaspoon instant coffee powder
1/2 teaspoon vanilla extract
8 pecan halves, to decorate

FOR THE ICING
175g butter, softened
100g icing sugar
1 teaspoon instant coffee powder
4 tablespoons maple syrup

1. Preheat the oven to 180°C/350°F/Gas mark 4. Grease and line a deep 20cm round cake tin. For the cake, sift the flour and salt together three times into a bowl and set aside. Melt the butter and set aside.

2. Using a hand-held electric mixer, whisk the eggs and sugar together in a large, heat-proof bowl set over a pan of simmering water, until the mixture is pale, creamy and thick enough to leave a trail on the surface when the whisk is lifted.

3. In a small bowl, dissolve the coffee in 1 tablespoon of hot water, then whisk this into the egg mixture together with the vanilla extract. Sift the flour over the egg mixture in three batches, drizzling a little melted butter around the edge of the mixture in between each batch, and carefully fold in.

4. Pour the mixture evenly into the prepared tin. Bake in the oven for 25–30 minutes, or until risen and golden. Cool in the tin for 2–3 minutes, then turn out onto a wire rack and leave to cool completely.

5. For the icing, beat the butter and icing sugar together in a bowl until smooth. In a small bowl, dissolve the coffee in 1 tablespoon of hot water, then gradually beat this into the creamed mixture together with the maple syrup until smooth and well mixed.

6. Cut the cake in half horizontally twice to make three layers. Sandwich the cake layers together with some of the icing, then spread the remaining icing over the top and sides of the cake. Decorate the top with pecan halves.

LEMON & LIME LOVE Cake

This tangy loaf cake is known by lots of different names, but Love Cake is particularly appropriate as everyone who tries it finds it impossible to resist!

MAKES: 12–14 SLICES

175g plain flour
2 teaspoons baking powder
½ teaspoon salt
75g unsalted butter, softened
275g caster sugar
2 eggs, lightly beaten
125ml milk
Finely grated zest of 1 lemon and juice of ½ lemon
Finely grated zest and juice of 1 lime

1. Preheat the oven to 170°C/325°F/Gas mark 3. Grease and flour a 900g loaf tin. Sift the flour, baking powder and salt into a large bowl.

2. Put the butter in a separate bowl and add 175g of the sugar. Beat together until pale and fluffy, then gradually beat in the eggs, adding a little flour if the mixture shows any sign of curdling. Gradually add the remaining flour, alternating with the milk and beating well after each addition. Stir in the lemon and lime zests.

3. Spoon the mixture into the prepared tin and level the surface. Bake in the oven for 40–50 minutes, or until a skewer inserted into the centre comes out clean. Turn out onto a wire rack.

4. Mix the lemon and lime juices with the remaining sugar in a bowl. Put a tray underneath the wire rack and spoon the sugar mixture evenly over the top of the cake, letting it run down the sides slightly. Allow the cake to cool completely before serving in slices.

TURKISH FIG & SESAME Cake

A very more-ish cake that has Middle Eastern flavours. It is ideal for lunch boxes, but it also makes a lovely dessert when served with yoghurt.

MAKES: 16 SQUARES

5 eggs, separated
225g caster sugar
Finely grated zest of 1 lime
100g semolina
100g ground almonds
200g ready-to-eat dried figs, chopped
2 tablespoons sesame seeds

FOR THE SYRUP
Juice of 2 limes
90g caster sugar

1. Preheat the oven to 190°C/375°F/Gas mark 5. Grease and base line a deep 23cm square cake tin.

2. For the cake, using a hand-held electric mixer, whisk the egg yolks, sugar and lime zest together in a bowl until the mixture is very thick and creamy. Fold in the semolina and ground almonds. In a separate bowl, whisk the egg whites until stiff, then fold one-third of the whisked whites into the almond mixture to loosen it. Fold in the remaining whisked egg whites until well combined.

3. Pour the mixture evenly into the prepared tin and scatter the chopped figs over the surface. Sprinkle the sesame seeds over the top. Bake in the oven for about 30 minutes, or until firm to the touch.

4. Meanwhile, make the syrup. Put the lime juice, 5 tablespoons of cold water and the sugar in a saucepan and bring to the boil, stirring. Boil for about 2–3 minutes, or until syrupy. Remove the pan from the heat.

5. Remove the cake from the oven and prick the top surface all over with a skewer or fork. Pour the hot syrup evenly over the hot cake, then leave the cake in the tin to cool completely. Once cold, turn out and serve in slices or squares.

BANOFFEE Cheesecake

MAKES: 10–12 SLICES

225g plain flour
Pinch of salt
100g unsalted butter, diced
50g caster sugar

FOR THE FILLING

115g dark bitter chocolate, broken
    into squares and melted
3 large ripe but firm bananas
Juice of ½ lemon
250g mascarpone cheese
150ml whipping cream, lightly
    whipped
450g jar thick toffee or caramel
    sauce/spread

1. For the pastry, sift the flour into a bowl with the salt. Rub in the butter until the mixture resembles coarse breadcrumbs. Stir in the sugar. Add 3 tablespoons of cold water and mix to a dough. Turn the dough onto a lightly floured surface and knead briefly until the dough is smooth. Shape into a ball, wrap in cling film and refrigerate for 20 minutes.

2. On a lightly floured surface, roll out the pastry to form a rough circle at least 5cm larger than a loose-bottomed 23cm fluted tart tin set on a baking sheet. Use the pastry circle to line the tin, pressing the pastry into the edges and trimming any overhanging pastry. Prick the base all over with a fork. Refrigerate for 20 minutes.

3. Meanwhile, preheat the oven to 200°C/400°F/Gas mark 6. Line the pastry case with greaseproof paper and baking beans and bake in the oven for 12 minutes. Remove the baking beans and paper and bake for a further 10–12 minutes, or until golden. Remove from the oven and set aside to cool.

4. Using a pastry brush, paint the melted chocolate onto the inside of the pastry to cover completely. Chill until set.

5. To assemble the cheesecake, peel and thickly slice the bananas, then toss them in the lemon juice. Set aside. Beat the mascarpone cheese in a bowl until softened, then stir in the whipped cream. Carefully fold the cream mixture and most of the toffee or caramel sauce/spread together (reserving a little sauce/spread for decoration), but don't over-mix – leave them marbled. Spoon the mixture evenly into the pastry case, then scatter the banana slices over the top. Drizzle the remaining toffee or caramel sauce/spread decoratively over the bananas. Serve in slices.

LEMON & POPPY SEED POUND Cake

This poppy seed cake is soaked with a tangy lemon syrup after it has been baked to give a superbly moist texture and delicious taste. It will keep well in an airtight container for up to 1 week.

MAKES: 12–14 SLICES

175g unsalted butter, softened
175g caster sugar
3 eggs, beaten
175g self-raising flour
1 tablespoon poppy seeds
2 teaspoons finely grated lemon zest

FOR THE SYRUP

3 tablespoons granulated sugar
Juice of 1 lemon

CAKE TIP

To squeeze the maximum juice from a lemon, make sure it is at room temperature and roll it under your palm on a work surface to soften the fruit and get the juices flowing.

1. Preheat the oven to 180°C/350°F/Gas mark 4. Grease and base line a 900g loaf tin.

2. For the cake, cream the butter and sugar together in a bowl until light and fluffy. Gradually beat in the eggs, beating well after each addition, then fold in the flour, poppy seeds and lemon zest.

3. Turn the mixture into the prepared tin and level the surface. Bake in the oven for $1\frac{1}{4}$–$1\frac{1}{2}$ hours, or until risen and golden and a skewer inserted into the centre comes out clean. Remove the cake from the oven but leave it in the tin.

4. To make the syrup, gently heat the sugar and lemon juice together in a saucepan, stirring until the sugar has dissolved. Bring to the boil, then remove the pan from the heat and pour the hot syrup over the hot cake. Leave the cake to cool completely in the tin, then turn out and serve in slices.

PISTACHIO, YOGHURT & CARDAMOM Cake

This cake has wonderful scented Middle Eastern flavours and is ideal for picnics and packed lunches.

MAKES: 6–8 SLICES

150g pistachio nuts
Seeds from 8 cardamom pods, crushed
150g unsalted butter
175g self-raising flour
175g caster sugar
3 eggs, beaten
125g whole milk natural yoghurt
1 teaspoon almond extract
Extra whole pistachio nuts, for decoration

CAKE TIP
To bring out the flavour of pistachios, spread them on a baking sheet and toast them in an oven preheated to 140°C/300°F/Gas mark 2 for 5–10 minutes until just fragrant.

1. Preheat the oven to 180°C/350°F/Gas mark 4. Grease and base line a deep 18cm round cake tin.

2. Put the pistachio nuts and cardamom seeds in a blender or food processor and process until finely chopped. Add the butter, flour and sugar and pulse for about 20 seconds. Add the eggs, yoghurt and almond extract and pulse until just combined.

3. Spoon the mixture into the prepared tin and level the surface. Sprinkle the whole pistachio nuts over the top.

4. Bake in the oven for about 45–60 minutes, or until well risen, firm to the touch and a skewer inserted into the centre comes out clean. Cool in the tin for 5–10 minutes, then turn out onto a wire rack and leave to cool completely. Serve in slices.

CHERRY Cheesecake

MAKES: 10–12 SLICES

300g plain flour, sifted
100g icing sugar
150g unsalted butter
6 egg yolks
2 teaspoons finely grated lemon zest
2 tablespoons whipping cream
200g caster sugar
500g cream cheese or full fat soft
   cheese
Pinch of salt
3 tablespoons cornflour
2 eggs, beaten
250ml soured cream
2 teaspoons vanilla extract
425g can stoned cherries in syrup or
   fruit juice, drained

1. Grease a 23cm springform tin fitted with a flat base. Sift the flour, less 3 tablespoons, with the icing sugar into a bowl. Rub in 125g of the butter until the mixture resembles fine breadcrumbs. Add 4 egg yolks, the lemon zest and whipping cream and mix to form a dough. Shape into a ball, wrap in greaseproof paper and refrigerate for 20 minutes. Preheat the oven to 190°C/375°F/Gas mark 5.

2. On a lightly floured surface, roll out the dough until it is 5mm thick. Line the base and three-quarters of the way up the sides of the prepared tin with the dough. Prick the base all over with a fork. Freeze for 10 minutes.

3. When the pastry case is firm, line it with greaseproof paper and baking beans. Bake blind in the oven for 10–12 minutes, then remove the baking beans and paper and bake for 3–5 minutes. Remove from the oven.

4. In a bowl, rub the remaining flour, butter and 25g of the caster sugar together to form coarse crumbs, then set aside.

5. Beat the cream cheese or soft cheese in a separate bowl until smooth. Add the salt, cornflour and remaining caster sugar and beat for 1 minute. Gradually add the eggs and remaining egg yolks, beating well to combine. Stir in the soured cream and vanilla extract, mixing well. Fold in the cherries, then spoon the mixture into the pastry case and level the surface.

6. Sprinkle the reserved crumb topping mixture over the top. Bake in the oven for 20 minutes, then reduce the oven temperature to 150°C/300°F/Gas mark 2 and bake for a further 30–35 minutes. Turn off the oven and leave the cheesecake inside to cool for 30 minutes. Remove from the oven and set aside to cool completely, then refrigerate before serving.

ICED LIME Traybake

The crunchy topping is just as delicious if you use lemon or orange juice in place of the lime juice. The secret is to pour it over while the cake is still hot so the juice soaks in and the sugar forms a crunchy topping as it cools.

MAKES: 6–8 SQUARES

225g unsalted butter, softened
225g caster sugar
225g self-raising flour
1 teaspoon baking powder
4 large eggs
2 teaspoons finely grated lime zest
10–12 sugar cubes, crushed

FOR THE TOPPING
Thinly pared zest of 2 limes and the
    juice of 3 limes
100g granulated sugar

1. Preheat the oven to 180°C/350°F/Gas mark 4. Lightly grease and line an 28 x 18cm cake tin or baking tin.

2. For the cake, put all the ingredients except the crushed sugar cubes into a large bowl and beat together until smooth, light and well mixed. Turn the mixture into the prepared tin and level the surface. Sprinkle the crushed sugar cubes evenly over the top.

3. Bake in the oven for 40 minutes, or until well risen, golden and the top springs back when lightly pressed.

4. Mix the topping ingredients together in a bowl. Remove the cake from the oven and pour the sugar topping evenly over the cake. Leave the cake to cool completely in the tin, then turn out and cut into slices or squares to serve.

SPECIAL
OCCASION
CAKES

MOTHER'S DAY Cake

A pretty spring cake for Mother's Day, easy enough for kid's to make
or at least lend a helping hand.

MAKES: **12–16 SLICES**

300g plain flour
300g caster sugar
200g soft margarine
175ml milk
3 eggs, beaten
2½ teaspoons baking powder
1 teaspoon vanilla extract

FOR THE ICING
2 lemons
500g icing sugar, sifted
125g soft margarine
A few drops of yellow food colouring
Small artificial, fresh or sugar flowers
    such as daisies or pansies, to
    decorate

1. Preheat the oven to 180°C/350°F/Gas mark 4. Grease and flour a
30cm round pizza tin with a 1.5cm-high rim. Grease and flour a 1.1-litre
heat-proof pudding basin.

2. Put all the cake ingredients into a bowl and, using a hand-held electric
mixer, beat together until smooth. Spoon just under half of the cake
mixture into the prepared basin and level the surface, then spread the
rest of the cake mixture in the prepared pizza tin.

3. Place in the oven and bake the pizza tin cake for about 15 minutes and
the bowl cake for about 50 minutes, or until risen and golden brown and a
skewer inserted into the centre of the bowl cake comes out clean. Leave to
cool in the tin and basin for 5 minutes, loosen the bowl cake with a round-
bladed knife, then turn both cakes onto a wire rack and leave to cool.

4. To make the icing, finely grate the zest from one of the lemons and
squeeze the juice from both. Put the lemon zest and juice into a bowl,
add the icing sugar and margarine and beat together until smooth. Add a
few drops of yellow food colouring to give the icing a pale yellow tint.

5. Place the hat brim (pizza cake) on a cake board. If the top of the bowl
cake is rounded, trim it flat with a knife. Attach the flat side of the bowl cake
to the centre of the pizza cake using a little icing. Spread the remaining icing
all over the cake using a palette knife, covering the cake completely.
Decorate with artificial, fresh or sugar flowers and serve in slices.

VALENTINE Cake

Don't keep this cake just for Valentine's day – a heart shape is good for an engagement party or even a girl's birthday, just use pink icing, candles and sparkly ribbon.

MAKES: 16 SLICES

225g soft margarine
225g golden caster sugar
4 eggs, beaten
200g self-raising flour
25g unsweetened cocoa powder, sifted
100g plain chocolate, melted

FOR THE TOPPING & ICING
175g soft margarine
350g icing sugar, sifted
4 tablespoons unsweetened cocoa powder, sifted
750g poppy-red ready-to-roll fondant icing
Sugar roses and ribbon, to decorate

1. Preheat the oven to 180°C/350°F/ Gas mark 4. Grease and base line a 26 x 26cm heart-shaped tin.

2. For the cake, beat the margarine and sugar together in a bowl until light and fluffy. Add the eggs, flour, cocoa powder and melted chocolate and beat together until smooth and well mixed. Spoon the mixture into the prepared tin and level the surface.

3. Bake in the oven for 35–40 minutes, or until a skewer inserted into the centre comes out clean. Cool in the tin for 5 minutes, then turn out onto a wire rack and leave to cool completely.

4. To make the topping, cream the margarine and one third of the icing sugar together in a bowl. Gradually beat in the remaining icing sugar and the cocoa powder, mixing well.

5. Spread the chocolate icing evenly over the top and sides of the cake. Roll out the red fondant icing and use it to cover the cake. Decorate as desired with sugar roses and ribbon. Serve in slices.

MOLASSES Gingerbread

This rich gingerbread is perfect served at a Halloween party – it's really a hybrid of a cake and a teabread and is delicious served in slices spread with unsalted butter.

MAKES: 8–10 SQUARES

400g plain flour
1 teaspoon baking powder
1 tablespoon ground ginger
1 teaspoon ground cinnamon
225g unsalted butter
125g molasses or black treacle
175g soft light or dark brown sugar
3 eggs, beaten
75g glacé cherries, halved
115g stoned dried dates, chopped
55g preserved stem ginger, drained
  and chopped
90g sultanas

1. Preheat the oven to 150°C/300°F/Gas mark 2. Grease and line a deep 20cm square cake tin.

2. Sift the flour, baking powder, ground ginger and cinnamon into a large bowl. Set aside.

3. Place the butter in a saucepan with the molasses or black treacle and sugar and stir over a low heat until melted. Pour the melted mixture into the flour mixture and stir to mix well. Beat in the eggs until smooth, then stir in the glacé cherries, dates, stem ginger and sultanas, mixing well.

4. Pour the mixture evenly into the prepared tin. Bake in the oven for 1–1¼ hours, or until a skewer inserted into the centre comes out clean. Cool in the tin for 5 minutes, then turn out onto a wire rack and leave to cool completely. Serve in slices.

CAKE TIP

To measure molasses easily, stand the tin in a bowl containing hot water for a few minutes. The molasses will become runny and less sticky,

GREEK EASTER Cake

MAKES: 6–8 SLICES

125g unsalted butter, softened
100g caster sugar
Finely grated zest of 1 lemon
1 tablespoon lemon juice
2 eggs, beaten
125g semolina
2 teaspoons baking powder
100g ground almonds
Greek-style yoghurt, to serve
   (optional)
FOR THE SYRUP
10 cardamom pods
1 orange
300g caster sugar
Juice of ½ lemon
2 small cinnamon sticks
1 teaspoon whole cloves
2 tablespoons orange flower water

CAKE TIP
This beautiful sweet-scented cake also makes a lovely summer dessert when served with fresh orange slices.

1. Preheat the oven to 180°C/350°F/Gas mark 4. Grease and base line an 18cm springform cake tin fitted with a flat base.

2. For the cake, cream the butter and sugar together in a bowl until pale and fluffy. Add the lemon zest, lemon juice, eggs, semolina, baking powder and ground almonds and mix well until smooth. Turn the mixture into the prepared tin and level the surface.

3. Bake in the oven for about 45 minutes, or until just firm to the touch. Leave in the tin for a few minutes, then loosen and turn out onto a wire rack. Remove the lining paper. Clean the tin, then place the very warm cake back into it.

4. While the cake is baking, make the syrup. Lightly crush the cardamom pods. Pare the rind from the orange and cut it into fine strips. Squeeze the juice from the orange and reserve.

5. Put the sugar and 200ml water in a small saucepan and heat gently until the sugar dissolves. Add the lemon juice and boil rapidly for about 3 minutes, or until syrupy. Add the orange strips, orange juice, cardamom, cinnamon sticks and cloves and cook gently for 5 minutes. Remove the pan from the heat and stir in the orange-flower water.

6. Spoon some of the syrup over the very warm cake in the tin. When it has been absorbed, spoon over some more until the cake is steeped in syrup. Set aside to cool in the tin completely, then chill until ready to serve. Remove the cake from the tin and serve in slices (discarding the decorative spices), with syrup from around the cake spooned over. Serve topped with Greek-style yoghurt, if you like.

EASTER Cake

MAKES: 12–14 SLICES

500g luxury mixed dried fruit
2 tablespoons Amaretto
175g unsalted butter, softened
175g soft light brown sugar
3 eggs, beaten
Finely grated zest of ½ lemon
200g self-raising flour
2 teaspoons ground mixed spice
50g ground almonds
500g ready-made natural almond
   paste or marzipan
225g ready-made yellow almond
   paste or marzipan
1–2 tablespoons apricot jam, warmed
Coloured ribbon and mall chocolate
   or sugar-coated eggs, to decorate

1. Put the mixed dried fruit in a bowl and sprinkle over the Amaretto. Leave to soak for 1 hour. Preheat the oven to 150°C/300°F/Gas mark 2. Grease and line a deep 18cm round cake tin.

2. Cream the butter and sugar together in a bowl. Beat in the eggs and lemon zest. Fold in the flour, mixed spice and ground almonds, then add the dried fruit mixture and mix well. Set aside.

3. Roll out half of the natural almond paste or marzipan on a sheet of non-stick baking paper to form an 18cm circle. Spoon half of the cake mixture into the base of the prepared tin, spreading it evenly. Place the almond paste circle on top. Spoon over the remaining cake mixture, then level the surface. Bake in the oven for 2–2¼ hours, or until a skewer inserted into the centre comes out clean. Turn out onto a wire rack to cool.

4. Roll out the remaining natural almond paste and all but 50g of the yellow paste to form two 18cm circles and place the yellow one on top of the natural one. Shape 8 balls from the remaining yellow paste.

5. Lightly brush the top of the cake with warm jam, leaving a small circle in the centre uncoated. Place the almond circle, yellow-side up, on top of the cake and trim the edges. Using a glass, lightly mark a circle in the centre of the cake. Using a sharp knife, cut through both almond-paste layers up to the edges of the circle to make 8 segments. Lift up the pointed end of each segment and peel it back to reveal the natural almond paste underside. Press it gently into the edge of the cake. Place a yellow almond paste ball on top.

6. Tie a ribbon around the cake and fill the centre with sugar-coated chocolate eggs. Serve in slices.

NEW YORK Cheesecake

You can dress up or dress down this American classic.

Serve it plain or topped with fruit compote.

MAKES: 12–14 SLICES

200g digestive biscuits, crushed
50g unsalted butter, melted
900g cream cheese or full-fat soft
   cheese
Pinch of salt
300g caster sugar
250ml soured cream
2 teaspoons vanilla extract
1 tablespoon finely grated lemon zest
1 tablespoon lemon juice
4 eggs, beaten
2 egg yolks

1. Preheat the oven to 150°C/300°F/Gas mark 2. Grease a 23cm springform tin fitted with a flat base.

2. In a bowl, mix together the biscuit crumbs and melted butter, then press this mixture evenly into the base of the prepared tin. Bake in the oven for 10 minutes, or until lightly browned, then remove from the oven and set aside to cool.

3. In a separate bowl, beat the cream cheese or soft cheese until soft and smooth. Add the salt and sugar and beat for 1 minute. Add the soured cream, vanilla extract, lemon zest and lemon juice and beat for a further 1 minute. Add the eggs and egg yolks and beat until well combined. Pour the mixture evenly over the biscuit base in the tin.

4. Bake in the oven for 45–50 minutes, or until the edges are set but the centre is still slightly soft. Turn off the oven, leave the cheesecake inside and leave the door ajar. Leave to cool in the oven for 45 minutes.

5. Remove the cheesecake from the oven and cool to room temperature. Remove from the tin, place on a serving plate, cover with foil and refrigerate for at least 4 hours or preferably overnight, before serving. Serve in slices.

PUMPKIN SPICE Cake

Rich and full-flavoured, this dark, spicy cake is great served with fresh cream at a Thanksgiving feast.

MAKES: 15 SLICES

300g plain flour
2 teaspoons bicarbonate of soda
Pinch of salt
3 teaspoons ground cinnamon
1 teaspoon freshly grated nutmeg
1½ teaspoons ground allspice
½ teaspoon ground ginger
300g unsalted butter, softened
200g soft light brown sugar
200g caster sugar
2 eggs, beaten
425g can pumpkin purée
200g pecans, chopped

1. Preheat the oven to 180°C/350°F/Gas mark 4. Grease, base line and flour a 25cm Bundt tin.

2. Sift the flour, bicarbonate of soda, salt and ground spices into a bowl and set aside. Cream the butter and sugars together in a separate bowl until pale and fluffy, then gradually beat in the eggs.

3. Beat in the pumpkin purée, then stir in the flour mixture and pecans, mixing well. Pour the mixture evenly into the prepared tin.

4. Bake in the oven for 50–60 minutes, or until a skewer inserted into the centre comes out clean. Cool in the tin for 10 minutes, then turn out onto a wire rack and leave to cool completely. Serve in slices.

CAKE TIP
For a lighter taste substitute puréed butternut squash for the pumpkin.

PANETTONE

MAKES: 8 SLICES

1 tablespoon dried yeast granules
150ml warmed milk
450g strong plain white flour
1 egg, beaten
4 egg yolks
2 teaspoons salt
75g caster sugar
2 teaspoons finely grated lemon zest
2 teaspoons finely grated orange zest
175g unsalted butter, softened
75g chopped mixed peel
100g raisins

CAKE TIP
This bread dough takes time to rise. Don't leave it in a very warm place once the butter has been incorporated or it will melt and the dough will be greasy.

1. Grease and line a 15cm round cake tin with a depth of 10cm with a double layer of greaseproof paper that is 12cm higher than the rim of the tin. In a large bowl, dissolve the yeast in 4 tablespoons of the warmed milk. Cover and leave in a warm place for about 10 minutes, or until frothy. Stir in 100g of the flour and the remaining milk, mixing well. Cover and leave to rise in a warm place for about 30 minutes.

2. In a separate bowl, beat the egg and egg yolks together. Set aside. Sift the remaining flour and salt into the yeast mixture. Make a well in the centre and add the sugar, beaten eggs and lemon and orange zests, mixing to form a soft dough. Knead for about 5 minutes, or until smooth and elastic. Work in the butter until evenly incorporated.

3. Shape the dough into a ball and place in a clean oiled bowl. Cover and leave in a cool place to rise for 2–4 hours, or until doubled in size – the longer the better.

4. Preheat the oven to 200°C/400°F/Gas mark 6. Turn the dough onto a clean surface and knead in the mixed peel and raisins. Shape the dough into a neat ball and place it in the prepared tin. Cut a cross in the top with a sharp knife. Cover and leave to rise again until the dough is 2.5cm above the top of the tin.

5. Bake in the oven for 15 minutes, then reduce the oven temperature to 180°C/350°F/Gas mark 4 and bake for a further 40 minutes, or until well-risen and golden. Cool in the tin for 10 minutes, then turn out onto a wire rack and leave to cool completely. Serve in slices or wedges.

FESTIVE CHOCOLATE & HAZELNUT Roulade

This special dessert is really easy to make and can even be made the day before the celebration. Decorate with chocolate holly leaves before dusting with extra icing sugar.

MAKES: 6–8 SLICES

6 eggs, separated
150g caster sugar
50g unsweetened cocoa powder
Sifted icing sugar, for dusting
Decorations of your choice such as
    chocolate 'crisps' or holly leaves
    and holly decorations

FOR THE FILLING
250ml double or whipping cream
1 tablespoon brandy
50g toasted hazelnuts, finely chopped

1. Preheat the oven to 180°C/350°F/Gas mark 4. Grease and line a 29 x 18cm Swiss roll tin.

2. Whisk the egg yolks in a bowl until they start to thicken. Add the caster sugar and whisk until the mixture thickens slightly – don't let it get too thick. Sift the cocoa powder over the egg mixture and fold in lightly.

3. In a separate bowl, whisk the egg whites until they form stiff peaks. Using a metal spoon, fold the whisked egg whites into the egg yolk mixture. Pour the mixture evenly into the prepared tin.

4. Bake in the oven for 20–25 minutes, or until risen and springy to the touch. Remove from the oven and leave to cool in the tin. When cold, turn the cake out onto a sheet of greaseproof paper liberally dusted with sifted icing sugar. Peel off the lining paper.

5. For the filling whip the cream and brandy together in a bowl to form soft peaks, then fold in the hazelnuts. Spread the cream mixture evenly over the roulade. Use the sugar-dusted paper to help you roll up the roulade from one long side.

6. Transfer the roulade to a serving plate while it is still wrapped in the rolling paper. Remove the paper and sift extra icing sugar over the roulade, if you like. Decorate as desired and serve in slices.

EASY CHRISTENING Cake

MAKES: 10–12 SLICES

6 eggs
150g caster sugar
100g self-raising flour
50g plain flour
FOR THE FILLING & TOPPING
4 tablespoons strawberry or
   raspberry jam
150ml double cream
100g unsalted butter, softened
250g icing sugar
350g ready-to-roll fondant icing
TO DECORATE
Ribbon (colour of your choice)
Decoration of your choice for the
   centre of the top of the cake
Pink and/or blue sugared almonds

CAKE TIP
*To save time, the
sponges can be
frozen, unfilled, for
up to one month.*

1. Preheat the oven to 180°C/350°F/Gas mark 4. Grease, base line and flour two 20cm round sandwich cake tins.

2. For the cake, using a hand-held electric mixer, whisk the eggs in a bowl for about 2 minutes. Gradually add the caster sugar and whisk for a further 5 minutes, or until the mixture is pale, creamy and thick enough to leave a trail on the surface when the whisk is lifted. Sift the two flours together, then gently fold them into the egg mixture together with 2 tablespoons of hot water. Divide the mixture evenly between the prepared tins and level the surface.

3. Bake in the oven for 20–25 minutes or until golden brown, firm in the centre and slightly shrunk away from the sides of the tins. Cool in the tin for 5 minutes, then turn out onto a wire rack and leave to cool completely. When cold, spread one sponge cake with the jam. Whip the cream in a bowl until soft peaks form, then spread the cream over the jam. Place the other sponge cake on top.

4. In a separate bowl, beat the butter and icing sugar together until pale and fluffy, then spread this evenly over the top and sides of the cake. Using a piece of string, measure up one side, across the top and down the other side of the cake. Roll out the fondant icing to a circle with a diameter the size you have measured. Carefully lift the fondant icing onto the cake and smooth the top and sides with your hands.

5. For the decoration, tie the ribbon around the cake and place your chosen decoration in the centre. Scatter the top with sugared almonds.

VERY EASY CHRISTMAS Cake

This is a very colourful cake, packed full with fruit. You can also use
this mixture to make two or three small cakes to give as gifts.

MAKES: 20 SLICES

150g ready-to-eat dried apricots,
　chopped
150g red glacé cherries
150g green glacé cherries
150g raisins
150g mixed glacé fruits such as
　pineapple, lemon, ginger, etc.
50g pitted prunes, halved
50g Brazil nuts
50g pecans
100g ground almonds
3 eggs
50g butter, melted
70g plain flour
1/2 teaspoon baking powder
3 tablespoons clear honey
2 teaspoons vanilla extract

1. Preheat the oven to 150°C/300°F/Gas mark 2. Grease and line a 30 x 11cm loaf tin.

2. Put all the fruit, nuts and ground almonds into a bowl and mix together well. Set aside.

3. Using a hand-held electric mixer, whisk the eggs in a bowl until the mixture is pale, creamy and thick enough to leave a trail on the surface when the whisk is lifted. Whisk in the melted butter, flour, baking powder, honey and vanilla extract until combined, then pour this mixture onto the fruit mixture and stir to mix well.

4. Turn the mixture into the prepared tin and press down to level the surface. Bake in the oven for about 1½ hours, or until firm to the touch. Leave to cool in the tin, then turn out onto a wire rack and leave until cold. Serve in slices.

CREOLE CHRISTMAS Cake

This is a very rich, moist cake for those who love tradition. The preparation needs to be started a few days before making the cake.

MAKES: 30 SLICES

FOR PRE-SOAKING
5 tablespoons EACH rum, port, brandy, cherry brandy and water
1 teaspoon Angostura bitters
½ teaspoon ground cinnamon
½ teaspoon freshly grated nutmeg
½ teaspoon ground cloves
½ teaspoon ground allspice
¼ teaspoon salt
1 teaspoon vanilla extract
1 tablespoon molasses sugar or soft dark brown sugar
1kg luxury mixed dried fruit

FOR THE CAKE
225g unsalted butter, softened
225g demerara sugar
4 eggs, beaten
225g self-raising flour
50g lightly toasted pecans, chopped

TO DECORATE
About 4 tablespoons strained apricot jam
500g ready-made almond paste or marzipan
500g ready-made royal icing
Silver balls, etc.

1. Put all the ingredients for pre-soaking into a large saucepan. Bring to the boil and simmer gently for 10 minutes, stirring frequently. Remove the pan from the heat and set aside to cool. Put the cold fruit mixture in an airtight container and leave in the refrigerator for 7 days. Stir the mixture every day.

2. Preheat the oven to 140°C/275°F/Gas mark 1. Grease the base and sides of a deep 20cm square cake tin and double line it with non-stick baking paper.

3. For the cake, cream the butter and sugar together in a bowl. Add the eggs and flour and beat until smooth. Add all of the fruit mixture and the pecans and mix well. Spoon the mixture into the prepared tin and level the surface.

4. Cover the tin loosely with a double layer of greaseproof paper and bake in the oven for about 3½ hours, or until just cooked in the centre. Remove the cake from the oven and leave to cool completely in the tin, then remove and wrap in greaseproof paper and foil. Leave the wrapped cake in a cool, dry place for a week to allow it to mellow and firm before decorating.

5. To decorate the cake, brush the top and sides with apricot jam and cover with rolled-out almond paste or marzipan. Spread the royal icing over the top and sides of the cake and swirl decoratively using a palette knife. Add decorations, such as silver balls, as you like. Serve in slices.

CAKES
FOR KIDS

ICED SPONGE Cake

An apricot, sultana and almond topping completes
this delicious, light and moist sponge cake.

MAKES: 8–10 SLICES

250g plain flour
2 teaspoons baking powder
½ teaspoon salt
100g unsalted butter, softened
200g caster sugar
3 large eggs, beaten
1½ teaspoons vanilla extract
175ml milk
FOR THE ICING
4 egg whites
Pinch of cream of tartar
100g caster sugar
2 tablespoons chopped ready-to-eat
   dried apricots
2 tablespoons sultanas
2 tablespoons flaked almonds

1. Preheat the oven to 180°C/350°F/Gas mark 4. Grease and base line a
23cm round cake tin.

2. For the cake, sift the flour, baking powder and salt into a bowl. Set aside.
In a separate bowl, cream the butter and sugar together until light and fluffy.
Gradually add the eggs, beating well after each addition, then beat in the
vanilla extract. Fold in the flour mixture alternately with the milk; mix well.

3. Spoon the mixture into the prepared tin and level the surface. Bake in
the oven for 30–40 minutes, or until pale golden and a skewer inserted
into the centre comes out clean. Cool in the tin for 5 minutes, then turn
out onto a wire rack and leave to cool completely.

4. To make the icing, using a hand-held electric mixer, whisk the egg
whites and cream of tartar together in a bowl until stiff, then gradually
whisk in the sugar, until the mixture is stiff and glossy.

5. Place the cake on an ovenproof serving plate. Swirl the icing evenly
over the top of the cake, then sprinkle the top with the apricots, sultanas
and almonds. Return the cake to a warm oven for 4–5 minutes to give the
icing a little colour. Remove from the oven and set aside to cool. Serve in
slices and eat on day of making.

BAKED ALASKA
BIRTHDAY Cake

Dim the lights and light the candles. This is an all-time favourite celebration cake and the fresh raspberries make it extra special.

MAKES: 6–8 SLICES

175g unsalted butter, softened
175g granulated sugar
3 eggs, beaten
1 teaspoon vanilla extract
175g self-raising flour, sifted
350g raspberry jam
225g fresh raspberries
4 egg whites
225g caster sugar
8 scoops of vanilla or your favourite
   ice cream
Candles or sparklers, to decorate
   (optional)

1. Preheat the oven to 180°C/350°F/Gas mark 4. Grease and base line a deep 20cm round cake tin.

2. Cream the butter and granulated sugar together in a large bowl until pale and fluffy. Gradually add the eggs, beating well after each addition, then beat in the vanilla extract. Fold in the flour, mixing well.

3. Spoon the mixture into the prepared tin and level the surface. Bake in the oven for 30–35 minutes, or until risen and golden. Turn out onto a wire rack and leave to cool.

4. Increase the oven temperature to 220°C/425°F/Gas mark 7. Cut the sponge cake in half horizontally. Place the base sponge round on a baking sheet and spread with the jam. Place the second sponge round on top. Arrange the raspberries on top of the sponge cake.

5. Whisk the egg whites in a large bowl until they form stiff peaks. Slowly whisk in the caster sugar to make a thick, glossy meringue mixture.

6. Place scoops of ice cream over the raspberries to cover. Spread the meringue mixture evenly over the ice cream and sides of the sponge so that everything is covered. Bake in the oven for 8–10 minutes. Remove from the oven, decorate with birthday candles or sparklers, if using, and serve immediately in slices.

CHOCOLATE PEANUT BUTTER Cake

MAKES: 20 SLICES

225g unsalted butter, softened
225g soft light brown sugar
125g chunky peanut butter
125g plain chocolate, melted
225g plain flour
2 teaspoons baking powder
½ teaspoon bicarbonate of soda
4 eggs, beaten
5 tablespoons milk

FOR THE GLAZE & DECORATION
25g butter
2 tablespoons smooth peanut butter
3 tablespoons golden syrup
1 teaspoon vanilla extract
175g plain chocolate chips
30g icing sugar
150g plain chocolate, broken into
    squares
Chocolate-coated peanuts (optional)

1. Preheat the oven to 180°C/350°F/Gas mark 4. Grease and base line a flat-bottomed 25cm ring tin.

2. For the cake, beat the butter and sugar together in a bowl until light and fluffy. Beat in the peanut butter and melted chocolate. Sift the flour, baking powder and bicarbonate of soda into a separate bowl. Beat the eggs into the creamed mixture a little at a time, adding a little flour if the mixture shows any sign of curdling. Fold in the remaining flour and milk, mixing well. Turn the mixture into the prepared tin and level the surface.

3. Bake in the oven for about 50 minutes, or until a skewer inserted into the centre comes out clean. Cool in the tin for a few minutes, then turn out onto a wire rack and leave to cool completely.

4. To make the glaze, put the butter, peanut butter, golden syrup and vanilla extract into a saucepan. Heat gently until the butter has melted, stirring. Add the chocolate chips and stir until completely melted and smooth. Stir in the icing sugar. Remove the pan from the heat and leave to cool until it is of a thick pouring consistency.

5. Meanwhile, melt the plain chocolate and spread it evenly on a baking sheet lined with non-stick baking paper. Chill until almost set. Using a small star-shaped biscuit cutter, stamp out stars in the set chocolate. Leave until completely set and then lift them off the paper.

6. Pour the glaze evenly over the cake and decorate with chocolate stars and chocolate-coated peanuts, if using. Serve in slices.

ROCKY ROAD Cake

Mini marshmallows, walnuts and chocolate caramels make a
rich icing for this all-time favourite cake.

MAKES: 8–10 SLICES

225g self-raising flour
2 teaspoons baking powder
4 tablespoons unsweetened cocoa
   powder
Pinch of salt
225g unsalted butter, softened
250g caster sugar
4 eggs, beaten
6 tablespoons buttermilk
2 teaspoons vanilla extract
FOR THE FILLING & TOPPING
35 chocolate-covered caramels
3 tablespoons milk
125g mini marshmallows
100g walnuts, chopped

CAKE TIP
*Top the iced cake with
any decorations or your
choice, such as chopped
chocolate-covered caramels,
milk chocolate buttons,
marshmallows and/or
hazelnuts an pecans.*

1. Preheat the oven to 180°C/350°F/Gas mark 4. Grease and base line
two 20cm round sandwich cake tins.

2. For the cake, sift the flour, baking powder, cocoa powder and salt into
a bowl. In a separate bowl, beat the butter until pale and fluffy. Add the
sugar and beat for a further 2 minutes. Gradually add the eggs, beating
well after each addition, then stir in the buttermilk and vanilla extract.

3. Stir in the dry ingredients, mixing well. Spoon the mixture into the
prepared tins, dividing it evenly, and level the surface. Bake in the oven for
30–35 minutes, or until firm to the touch. Turn the cakes out onto a wire
rack and leave to cool.

4. Cut small slits into the top of each sponge cake and set aside. For the
filling and topping, put the chocolate caramels in a saucepan with the
milk and 25g of the marshmallows and heat gently until melted, stirring.
Put one sponge cake on a plate and pour over half of the melted
chocolate mixture. Sprinkle over half of the walnuts.

5. Place the second sponge cake on top and pour over the remaining
chocolate mixture. Sprinkle with the remaining marshmallows and
walnuts. Serve in slices.

MARBLE Cheesecake

This is a great cheesecake to serve for kids with it's attractive swirl of chocolate – who could resist.

MAKES: 12–14 SLICES

200g digestive biscuit crumbs
4 tablespoons unsalted butter, melted
3 (225g) packages cream cheese
Pinch salt
3 tablespoons cornflour
200g sugar
2 eggs
2 egg yolks
2 teaspoons vanilla extract
480ml whipping cream
150g dark chocolate, melted
4 tablespoons unsweetened cocoa powder
2 teaspoons vanilla seeds

1. Preheat the oven to 300°F/150°C/Gas mark 2. Grease a 23cm springform cake tin.

2. Mix together the digestive biscuit crumbs and melted butter, and press into the base of the prepared tin. Bake for 10 minutes, or until lightly browned, then leave to cool.

3. Beat the cheese until smooth. Add the salt, cornflour and sugar, and beat for 1 minute. Gradually add the eggs, beating to combine. Stir in the vanilla. Whip the cream, and fold into the mixture. Divide the mixture equally between two bowls. Add the melted chocolate and cocoa to one and mix well. Stir the vanilla seeds into the other bowl.

4. Spoon half the chocolate mixture into the tin then spoon the vanilla mix over the top. Spoon over the remaining chocolate mix and draw a knife through the mix to create a swirled marble effect.

5. Bake for 55–60 minutes, or until set at the edge but slightly soft in the centre. Turn off the oven and cool in the oven for 45 minutes.

6. Remove the cheesecake from the oven and cool to room temperature. Remove from the tin, cover with foil and refrigerate until cold.

COCONUT CREAM Cake

A tasty classic – add to the kids' lunch boxes or indulge yourself.

MAKES: 8–10 SLICES

125g unsalted butter, softened
150g caster sugar
250ml buttermilk
1 teaspoon vanilla extract
200g plain flour
1 teaspoon baking powder
½ teaspoon bicarbonate of soda
Pinch of salt
100g flaked or desiccated coconut
4 egg whites

CAKE TIP

To revive dry coconut flakes, cover with milk and refrigerate for a couple of hours. Drain and pat dry before using.

1. Preheat the oven to 180°C/350°F/Gas mark 4. Grease and base line a deep 23cm round cake tin.

2. Cream the butter and sugar together in a bowl until pale and fluffy, then mix in the buttermilk and vanilla extract. Sift the flour, baking powder, bicarbonate of soda and salt into the bowl and fold in until combined. Add the coconut, less 2 tablespoons, and mix well.

3. In a separate bowl, whisk the egg whites until stiff. Stir one third of the whisked egg whites into the cake mixture to loosen it, then fold in the remainder. Pour the mixture evenly into the prepared tin and sprinkle with the reserved 2 tablespoons of coconut.

4. Bake in the oven for 30–35 minutes, or until golden and firm to the touch. Turn out onto a wire rack and leave to cool. Serve in slices.

PINK & WHITE Cake

MAKES: 16 SLICES

FOR THE PLAIN CAKE
175g white vegetable fat or soft
   margarine
175g caster sugar
3 eggs, beaten
175g self-raising flour

FOR THE PINK CAKE
175g white vegetable fat or soft
   margarine
175g caster sugar
3 eggs, beaten
175g self-raising flour
Pink paste food colouring

FOR THE ICING & DECORATION
500g soft margarine
1kg icing sugar, sifted
Pink paste food colouring
Cake candles, to decorate

1. Preheat the oven to 180°C/350°F/Gas mark 4. To make the plain cake, grease and base line two 20cm round sandwich cake tins.

2. Beat the fat and sugar together in a bowl until light and creamy. Add the eggs and flour and beat until smooth. Divide the mixture evenly between the prepared tins and level the surface. Bake in the oven for 20–25 minutes, or until risen and firm to the touch. Cool in the tins for a few minutes, then turn out onto a wire rack and leave to cool completely.

3. To make the pink cakes, follow the same method as for the plain cakes but add some pink paste food colouring to the fat and sugar mixture, mixing well. Bake and cool the cakes as above.

4. To make the icing, put the margarine into a bowl and gradually beat in the icing sugar. Add some pink paste food colouring, mixing well.

5. To assemble the cakes, place them on a large work surface. Using a 12cm and a 5.5cm plain round biscuit cutter, cut rings from each cake. Carefully lift the central ring from each cake and replace it with one of the other colour. Spread a little icing over each cake and stack them on top of one another, making sure you alternate the cakes to give a chequerboard effect.

6. Spread a little of the icing over the top of the cake. Using a piping bag fitted with a star nozzle, pipe lines of icing down the sides of the cake and around the top edge. Arrange candles on top of the cake in the centre and pipe the remaining icing decoratively in a circle around them. Serve in slices.

MARSHMALLOW JAM Surprise

With marshmallows on top and a surprise layer of jam inside, this cake is great to make when friends come to tea.

MAKES: 8–10 SLICES

125g soft margarine
125g caster sugar
125g self-raising flour
2 eggs, beaten
2–3 tablespoons black cherry jam or any red jam of your choice
100g large white or pink marshmallows
175g icing sugar

1. Preheat the oven to 180°C/350°F/Gas mark 4. Grease and base line a deep 18cm round cake tin. Put the margarine, sugar, flour and eggs into a bowl and beat together until smooth and well mixed.

2. Spread half of the mixture into the base of the prepared tin. Dot with the jam. Spread the remaining cake mixture evenly over the top. Bake in the oven for about 40–45 minutes, or until well risen and golden brown.

3. While the cake is cooking, cut the marshmallows in half horizontally, using wetted scissors. Remove the cake from the oven and leave to cool in the tin for a few minutes, then turn out onto a wire rack. Cool the cake for about 15 minutes, then arrange the marshmallows, cut-side down, over the top of the warm cake (the cake needs to be warm enough for the cut sides of the marshmallows to melt slightly so that they stick to the cake). Leave the cake until quite cold.

4. Mix together the icing sugar and enough water in a bowl to make a thick pouring consistency. Pour the icing over the cake and allow it to run slightly down the sides. Serve in slices.

CHOCOLATE RIPPLE Cake

Serve this cake thickly sliced to reveal the luscious chocolate ripples.

MAKES: 12–14 SLICES

200g plain chocolate, broken into squares
250g unsalted butter, softened
2 tablespoons soft light brown sugar
½ teaspoon ground cinnamon
200g caster sugar
3 eggs, beaten
2 teaspoons vanilla extract
200g self-raising flour
½ teaspoon baking powder
100g plain or milk chocolate chunks

CAKE TIP
When melting chocolate remember that the smaller the pieces the quicker and more evenly the chocolate will melt.

1. Preheat the oven to 180°C/350°F/Gas mark 4. Grease and base line a 900g loaf tin. Melt the plain chocolate with 50g of the butter in a heat-proof bowl set over a pan of simmering water. Remove the bowl from the heat and stir in the brown sugar and cinnamon. Set aside.

2. Beat the remaining butter and caster sugar together in a bowl until pale and fluffy. Add the eggs and vanilla extract, then sift the flour and baking powder into the bowl. Beat together until smooth and well mixed.

3. Spread one-quarter of the mixture into the base of the prepared tin. Spread one-third of the melted chocolate mixture over the cake mixture. Repeat the layering twice more, then finish with a layer of cake mixture spread evenly on top.

4. Sprinkle the chocolate chunks evenly over the top. Bake in the oven for about 45–60 minutes, or until a skewer inserted into the centre comes out clean. Cool in the tin for 5–10 minutes, then turn out onto a wire rack and leave to cool completely. Serve in slices.

CHOCO-MALT Cake

A great favourite for big and little kids, this cake goes well with a glass of milk, and with the addition of a few birthday candles, it makes a great party cake.

MAKES: 10–12 SLICES

225g soft margarine or softened butter
225g caster sugar
80g instant malted milk powder
50g unsweetened cocoa powder, sifted
4 eggs, beaten
200g self-raising flour, sifted
4 tablespoons milk

FOR THE ICING & DECORATION
4 tablespoons boiling water
50g instant malted milk powder
25g unsweetened cocoa powder
125g soft margarine or softened butter
250g icing sugar, sifted
Chocolate-coated malted milk balls, such as Maltesers, to decorate

1. Preheat the oven to 180°C/350°F/Gas mark 4. Grease and base line two 20cm round sandwich cake tins.

2. For the cake, cream the margarine or butter and sugar together in a bowl until blended. Add the malted milk powder, cocoa powder, eggs, flour and milk and beat together until smooth and creamy. Divide the mixture evenly between the prepared tins and level the surface.

3. Bake in the oven for about 30 minutes, or until well risen and firm to the touch. Cool in the tin for a few minutes, then turn out onto a wire rack and leave to cool completely.

4. To make the icing, blend the boiling water, malted milk powder and cocoa powder together in a bowl, then set aside to cool.

5. In a separate bowl, beat the margarine and half of the icing sugar together until creamy, then add the remaining icing sugar and the blended cocoa mixture, mixing well. Sandwich the two cakes together with half of the icing, then spread the remaining icing over the top. Scatter the chocolate-coated malted milk balls on top. Serve in slices.

JELLY BEAN Swiss Roll

This homemade sponge cake filled with your favourite jam is quick and easy to make – ideal for children's parties.

MAKES: 6–8 SLICES

100g self-raising flour
1½ teaspoons baking powder
Pinch of salt
3 eggs
150g caster sugar, plus 2 tablespoons
½ teaspoon vanilla extract
2 tablespoons semi-skimmed milk
6 tablespoons strawberry jam
50g unsalted butter, softened
125g icing sugar, sifted
Jelly beans, to decorate

CAKE TIP
Instead of jam, try lemon or orange curd, chocolate spread or even marshmallow cream.

1. Preheat the oven to 190°C/375°F/Gas mark 5. Grease and line a 28 x 23cm Swiss roll tin.

2. Sift the flour, baking powder and salt into a bowl and set aside. Using a hand-held electric mixer, whisk the eggs and 150g of the caster sugar together in a large bowl until the mixture is pale, creamy and thick enough to leave a trail on the surface when the whisk is lifted. Stir in the vanilla extract and milk.

3. Gently fold the dry ingredients into the egg mixture, then pour the mixture evenly into the prepared tin. Bake in the oven for 8–10 minutes, or until just firm to the touch.

4. Sprinkle a sheet of greaseproof paper with the remaining 2 tablespoons of caster sugar and turn the sponge out onto it. Peel away the lining paper, then roll up the sponge from a long side, with the greaseproof paper inside. Transfer to a wire rack and leave to cool for 10–15 minutes.

5. Unroll the sponge cake and discard the greaseproof paper, then spread the sponge evenly with strawberry jam and re-roll tightly. Beat the butter in a bowl until pale and fluffy, then beat in the icing sugar, mixing well. Using a piping bag fitted with a plain nozzle, pipe the butter icing over the Swiss roll and decorate with jelly beans.

ICED RASPBERRY Cake

For this simple and quick dessert, frozen raspberries are used straight from the freezer. Chill the cake well before serving.

MAKES: 8–10 SLICES

75g unsalted butter, melted
200g digestive biscuits, crushed
50g soft light brown sugar
175g raspberry jelly
300g frozen raspberries
20 large pink marshmallows
4 tablespoons milk
475ml whipping cream

CAKE TIP
An easy way to cut up jelly is to use wet kitchen scissors.

1. Preheat the oven to 180°C/350°F/Gas mark 4. Mix the melted butter, biscuit crumbs and sugar in a bowl, then press this mixture evenly into the base of a 23cm springform tin fitted with a flat base. Bake in the oven for 10 minutes, then remove from the oven and set aside to cool.

2. Dissolve the raspberry jelly in 125ml boiling water in a heat-proof jug or bowl, then stir in the frozen raspberries. Pour this mixture evenly over the prepared biscuit base in the tin. Set aside until the jelly is cool and set.

3. Place the marshmallows and milk in a saucepan and heat gently until melted, stirring. Pour into a heat-proof bowl and set aside to cool.

4. Whip the cream lightly in a separate bowl, then fold it through the cooled marshmallow mixture. Spoon the marshmallow cream on top of the raspberry jelly in the tin, spreading it evenly. Refrigerate for 2–3 hours before serving. Serve in slices.

CHOCOLATE CHIP & VANILLA Cake

For a simple tray bake use an oblong cake tin, but for something more fancy try using a 19 x 10cm Angel cake tin.

MAKES: 12–16 SLICES

225g soft margarine
225g caster sugar
225g self-raising flour
4 eggs, beaten
2 tablespoons milk
2 tablespoons unsweetened cocoa
   powder
2 tablespoons hot water
1 teaspoon vanilla extract
100g plain chocolate chips
100g white chocolate chips

1. Preheat the oven to 180°C/350°F/Gas mark 4. Grease and base line a 28 x 19cm cake tin.

2. Put the margarine, sugar, flour, eggs and milk into a bowl and beat together until smooth and well mixed. Spoon half of the mixture into a separate bowl. Mix the cocoa powder with the hot water in a small bowl and leave to cool slightly.

3. Mix the vanilla extract and 50g of the plain chocolate chips into one of the bowls of cake mixture. Place spoonfuls of this mixture randomly in the prepared tin.

4. Mix the blended cocoa and 50g of the white chocolate chips into the cake mixture in the second bowl. Spoon the chocolate mixture in between the plain mixture in the tin to fill in the gaps. Drag the handle of a teaspoon through the mixtures to create a marbled effect.

5. Bake in the oven for about 30 minutes, or until firm to the touch. Remove the cake from the oven and leave it to cool completely in the tin. Turn out the cake and place it on a serving plate. Melt the plain and white chocolate chips separately, then drizzle them decoratively over the top of the cake. Serve in slices.

HEDGEHOG Cake

Deceptively easy to make, this charming cake is ideal for a
small child's birthday party.

MAKES: 12–18 SLICES

200g self-raising flour
200g caster sugar
125g unsalted butter, softened
2 eggs, beaten
2 tablespoons drinking chocolate
   powder
5 tablespoons evaporated milk
5 tablespoons water

FOR THE ICING & DECORATION
125g unsalted butter, softened
225g icing sugar, sifted
2 tablespoons evaporated milk
125g ready-made almond paste or
   marzipan, tinted brown with food
   colouring
10–12 chocolate flake bars
1 red sugar-coated sweet
2 plain or milk chocolate chips

1. Preheat the oven to 180°C/350°F/Gas mark 4. Grease and base line a
900ml ovenproof round-bottomed glass pudding basin. Put all the cake
ingredients into a bowl and beat together well until light and fluffy.
Spoon the mixture into the prepared basin and level the surface, then
place the basin on a baking sheet.

2. Bake in the oven for about 1 hour, or until a skewer inserted into the
centre comes out clean. Cool in the basin for 5–10 minutes, loosen
around the edges of the cake with a round-bladed knife, then turn out
onto a wire rack and leave to cool completely.

3. To make the icing, beat the butter, icing sugar and evaporated milk
together in a bowl. Trim the top of the cake so it is flat, then place it cut-
side down and cut it in half vertically. Spread a little icing over the cut
sides of each half of the cake and join back together to make the semi-
circular hedgehog body.

4. Place the cake on a cake board. Mould the almond paste into a small
cone shape for the head and attach it to the body with a little icing. Spread
the remaining icing all over the body, covering it completely. Cut the
chocolate flakes into small 5cm lengths and push them into the icing at a
slight angle, to create the hedgehog spikes. Attach the red sweet on the tip
of the head for a nose and the chocolate chips for the eyes. Serve in slices.

PEPPERMINT-CHOCOLATE LAYER Cake

Crunchy peppermints top this minty, frosted
chocolate cake – a sure-fire favourite with kids.

MAKES: 10–12 SLICES

175g dark bitter chocolate, broken
   into squares
75g unsalted butter
500g caster sugar
3 egg yolks
350ml milk
300g self-raising flour
Pinch of salt
¼ teaspoon bicarbonate of soda
2 teaspoons vanilla extract

FOR THE ICING
3 egg whites
400g caster sugar
Pinch of salt
¼ teaspoon cream of tartar
2–3 drops of green food colouring
2–3 drops of peppermint flavouring
50g crushed peppermint sweets

1. Preheat the oven to 180°C/350°F/Gas mark 4. Grease and base line two 20cm round sandwich cake tins.

2. For the cake, melt the chocolate and butter in a large heat-proof bowl set over a pan of gently simmering water. Remove from the heat and leave to cool to room temperature. Stir in the sugar, then add the egg yolks and half of the milk and stir to mix well.

3. Add the flour, salt and bicarbonate of soda and beat for 1 minute using a hand-held electric mixer. Beat in the remaining milk and the vanilla extract. Spoon the mixture into the prepared tins, dividing it evenly, and level the surface.

4. Bake in the oven for 25–30 minutes, or until just firm to the touch. Turn out onto a wire rack and leave to cool.

5. To make the icing, mix the egg whites, sugar, salt, cream of tartar and 3 tablespoons of water in a heat-proof bowl set over a pan of gently simmering water. Whisk for about 7 minutes, or until the mixture forms firm peaks. Remove the bowl from the heat and stir in the food colouring and peppermint flavouring. Sandwich the two cakes together with some icing, then spread the remaining icing evenly over the top and sides of the cake. Decorate with the crushed sweets.

DESSERT
CAKES

WALNUT & STRAWBERRY Cake

MAKES: 8–10 SLICES

50g walnuts
4 eggs
100g caster sugar
75g plain flour, sifted
1 teaspoon baking powder

FOR THE ICING & DECORATION

1 egg white
175g caster sugar
A few drops of rose water
200g small strawberries, hulled
50g walnuts, finely chopped, to
    decorate

1. Preheat the oven to 180°C/350°F/Gas mark 4. Grease and base line a 20cm springform tin fitted with a flat base.

2. Process the walnuts in a blender or food processor until finely chopped – don't over-process or the nuts will become oily. Set aside.

3. Using a hand-held electric mixer, whisk the eggs and sugar together in a large heat-proof bowl set over a pan of simmering water, until pale, creamy and thick enough to leave a trail. Remove from the heat.

4. Sift the flour and baking powder over the egg mixture and fold in gently together with the processed walnuts until well mixed. Pour the mixture evenly into the prepared tin. Bake in the oven for 40–45 minutes, or until well risen, golden and just firm to the touch. Cool in the tin for 5 minutes, then turn out onto a wire rack and leave to cool completely.

5. To make the icing, put the egg white, sugar, 1 tablespoon of water and the rose water in a heat-proof bowl set over a pan of simmering water. Using a hand-held electric mixer, whisk the ingredients together for about 10–12 minutes, or until thick. Remove from the heat.

6. Up to 4 hours before serving, slice the cake in half horizontally. Sandwich the two cake halves together with a little icing and some sliced strawberries, reserving a few strawberries to decorate.

7. Spread the remaining icing over the top and sides of the cake. Halve the rest of the strawberries and arrange them on top of the cake. Press the chopped walnuts over the sides of the cake. Serve in slices.

SUMMER FRUIT Roulade

A light sponge cake encases sumptuous summer fruits and kirsch-flavoured whipped cream.

MAKES: 6–8 SLICES

5 large eggs, separated

140g caster sugar

75g creamed coconut (in a block), grated

225g frozen mixed summer fruits

1 tablespoon freshly squeezed orange juice

2 teaspoons cornflour

125ml double or whipping cream

2 teaspoons Kirsch

Sifted icing sugar, for dusting

2 tablespoons flaked or desiccated coconut

1. Preheat the oven to 180°C/350°F/Gas mark 4. Grease and base line a 33 x 23cm Swiss roll tin.

2. Whisk the egg yolks and caster sugar together in a bowl until thick and glossy. In a separate bowl, whisk the egg whites until they form stiff peaks. Fold the creamed coconut into the egg yolk mixture. Gently stir in half of the whisked egg whites, then fold in the rest. Pour the mixture evenly into the prepared tin.

3. Bake in the oven for about 20 minutes, or until risen and firm to the touch. Remove from the oven and leave to cool in the tin, covered with a wire rack and a clean damp tea towel.

4. Cook the summer fruits in a saucepan with the orange juice until the juices begin to run. Blend the cornflour with a little water and stir into the fruit. Cook until thickened, stirring, then remove the pan from the heat and set aside to cool. Whip the cream and kirsch together in a bowl to form soft peaks.

5. Liberally dust a piece of greaseproof paper with sifted icing sugar, then turn the sponge cake out onto it. Peel off the lining paper. Spread the cake evenly with the whipped cream and then the fruit.

6. Using the paper underneath to help, roll up the roulade from one long side. Transfer to a serving plate while it is still wrapped in the rolling paper. Remove the paper and sprinkle the roulade with flaked or desiccated coconut. Sift icing sugar on top. Serve in slices.

GOOEY CHOCOLATE Cake

Sheer, outrageous indulgence – this cake is deliciously gooey and melts in the mouth. It is utterly irresistible whatever the occasion!

MAKES: 8–10 SLICES

300g dark bitter chocolate (at least
   70% cocoa solids), broken into
   squares
175g unsalted butter
8 eggs, separated
200g soft light brown sugar
60g ground almonds
FOR THE TOPPING & DECORATION
125g plain chocolate, melted
125g milk chocolate, melted
Chocolate-dipped fresh strawberries,
   to decorate

1. Preheat the oven to 180°C/350°F/Gas mark 4. Grease a 20cm springform tin fitted with a flat base, then line the base and sides of the tin with foil.

2. For the cake, melt the chocolate and butter in a large, heat-proof bowl set over a pan of simmering water. Remove from heat and leave to cool.

3. In a separate bowl, whisk the egg yolks and sugar together until thick and pale. Stir in the cooled chocolate and butter mixture, then stir in the ground almonds.

4. In another bowl, whisk the egg whites until stiff, then fold them into the chocolate mixture. Pour the mixture evenly into the prepared tin. Place the tin in a roasting tin half full of boiling water.

5. Place in the oven and bake for 1–1¼ hours, or until the cake is quite firm, yet a skewer inserted into the centre comes out a little sticky. Remove the cake from the oven and leave to cool completely in the tin, then turn it out and place on a serving plate.

6. For the topping, drizzle the melted plain and milk chocolates decoratively over the cake. Decorate with chocolate-dipped strawberries and serve in slices.

HAZELNUT MERINGUE Cake

This rich yet light hazelnut meringue filled with bourbon-laced cream and fresh raspberries makes an impressive dinner party dessert. Fill the meringue about 1 hour before serving – any longer and it will start to go soft.

MAKES: 8–10 SLICES

4 egg whites
200g caster sugar
1 teaspoon vanilla extract
1 teaspoon cider vinegar
1 teaspoon cornflour
80g toasted hazelnuts, finely ground
2 tablespoons coarsely chopped
    toasted hazelnuts

FOR THE FILLING
75g natural yoghurt
2 tablespoons bourbon
2 tablespoons clear honey
125ml double or whipping cream
225g fresh raspberries
Sifted icing sugar, for dusting

1. Preheat the oven to 180°C/350°F/Gas mark 4. Grease and base line two 20cm round sandwich cake tins.

2. For the meringue, whisk the egg whites in a bowl until they form stiff peaks. Gradually whisk in the sugar to make a stiff and glossy meringue. Fold in the vanilla extract, vinegar, cornflour and ground hazelnuts.

3. Divide the mixture evenly between the two prepared tins and level the surface. Scatter the chopped hazelnuts over the top of one, then bake in the oven for 50–60 minutes, or until crisp. Turn out onto a wire rack and leave to cool.

4. For the filling, stir the yoghurt, bourbon and honey together in a bowl. In a separate bowl, whip the cream until it forms soft peaks, then fold into the yoghurt mixture together with the raspberries.

5. Sandwich the two meringues together with the cream mixture, with the nut-topped meringue uppermost. Dust with sifted icing sugar. Serve in slices.

CHOCOLATE & RASPBERRY Torte

MAKES: 10–12 SLICES

50g plain flour

4 tablespoons unsweetened cocoa
    powder, plus extra for dusting

3 large eggs

75g caster sugar

40g unsalted butter, melted

FOR THE FILLING

425ml double cream

4 tablespoons orange-flavoured
    liqueur

175g fresh or frozen and thawed
    raspberries

1 tablespoon icing sugar

50g plain chocolate, grated

1. Preheat the oven to 180°C/350°F/Gas mark 4. Grease and line a deep 23cm round cake tin. Sift the flour and cocoa powder into a bowl.

2. Using a hand-held electric mixer, whisk the eggs and caster sugar together in a large heat-proof bowl set over a pan of simmering water, until the mixture is pale, creamy and thick enough to leave a trail on the surface when the whisk is lifted. Remove from the heat.

3. In three batches, sift the flour and cocoa powder over the whisked egg mixture and gently fold in, drizzling a little melted butter around the edge of the bowl between each batch.

4. Pour the mixture evenly into the prepared tin. Bake in the oven for about 20 minutes, or until golden brown and the top springs back when lightly pressed. Cool in the tin for 2–3 minutes, then turn out onto a wire rack and leave to cool completely.

5. Whip the cream and liqueur together in a bowl to form soft peaks. Fold in the raspberries, icing sugar and chocolate.

6. Slice the cake in half horizontally. Grease and base line a 20cm springform tin fitted with a flat base and trim the cake to fit the base of the tin. Put one of the cake halves at the bottom of the tin. Pile in the raspberry cream, spreading it evenly, then top with the remaining cake half. Press down evenly and freeze for about 4 hours, or until the filling is firm.

7. Dust the top of the cake with sifted cocoa powder, then remove from the tin and serve in slices.

WHITE CHOCOLATE AMARETTO Cheesecake

MAKES: 10–12 SLICES

16–18 digestive biscuits
3–4 amaretti biscuits
50g unsalted butter, melted
½ teaspoon almond extract
½ teaspoon ground cinnamon
FOR THE FILLING
350g good-quality white chocolate,
   broken into squares
125ml double or whipping cream
675g cream cheese or full-fat soft
   cheese, softened
65g caster sugar
4 eggs
2 tablespoons Amaretto liqueur or
   ½ teaspoon almond extract
½ teaspoon vanilla extract
FOR THE TOPPING
400ml soured cream
50g caster sugar
1 tablespoon Amaretto or
   ½ teaspoon almond extract
White chocolate curls, to decorate

1. Preheat the oven to 180°C/350°F/Gas mark 4. Grease a 23cm springform tin fitted with a flat base. Put the biscuits in a blender or food processor and pulse into fine crumbs. Add the butter, almond extract and cinnamon and blend to mix. Press the mixture onto the base and sides of the prepared tin.

2. Bake in the oven for 5 minutes, then remove from the oven and transfer to a wire rack to cool. Reduce the temperature to 150°C/300°F/Gas mark 2.

3. For the filling, melt the chocolate and cream together in a saucepan over a low heat, stirring until smooth. Remove from the heat and set aside. Beat the cream cheese in a bowl until smooth. Gradually add the sugar, then each egg, beating well after each addition. Slowly beat in the melted chocolate mixture, Amaretto or almond extract and vanilla extract.

4. Spoon the mixture evenly over the biscuit base in the tin. Place the tin on a baking sheet and bake in the oven for 45–55 minutes, or until the edge of the cheesecake is firm, but the centre is slightly soft. Transfer to a wire rack. Increase the oven temperature to 200°C/400°F/Gas mark 6.

5. For the topping, beat the soured cream, sugar and Amaretto or almond extract together in a bowl. Spread evenly over the cheesecake and bake for 5–7 minutes. Turn off the oven, but leave the cheesecake inside for 1 hour, then transfer to a wire rack to cool. Run a sharp knife around the edge of the cheesecake, but leave in the tin. Refrigerate, loosely covered, overnight.

6. To serve, unclip and remove the cheesecake from the tin. Transfer to a serving plate and decorate with white chocolate curls. Serve in slices.

BLUEBERRY & WHITE CHOCOLATE
Meringue Roll

This is rather an unusual idea, using a meringue mixture to roll into a roulade-type dessert. The filling is a white chocolate cream with tangy, fragrant blueberries throughout.

MAKES: 10–12 SLICES

275g caster sugar
Seeds from ½ vanilla pod
5 egg whites
Sifted icing sugar, for dusting
150g white chocolate, broken into squares
100ml natural yoghurt
250g mascarpone cheese
100g fresh blueberries

CAKE TIP
For a lighter dessert use low fat soft cheese instead of mascarpone.

1. Preheat the oven to 220°C/425°F/Gas mark 7. Grease and line a 33 x 23cm Swiss roll tin.

2. Combine the caster sugar and vanilla seeds in a bowl. In a separate bowl, whisk the egg whites until stiff. Gradually whisk in the vanilla sugar, a spoonful at a time, to form a stiff, glossy meringue mixture.

3. Spread the meringue mixture evenly into the prepared tin. Bake in the oven for 8 minutes. Reduce the oven temperature to 170°C/325°F/Gas mark 3 and bake for a further 10 minutes, or until firm to the touch.

4. Turn out onto a sheet of greaseproof paper dusted with sifted icing sugar. Peel off the lining paper and set aside to cool for 10 minutes.

5. Meanwhile, melt the chocolate in a heat-proof bowl set over a pan of hot water. Remove from the heat and stir in the yoghurt, then beat this mixture into the mascarpone cheese in a separate bowl.

6. Spread the chocolate mixture over the meringue and top with the blueberries. Roll up from a long side using the paper underneath to help. Leave wrapped in the paper for at least 1 hour before serving. Remove the paper, dust with sifted icing sugar and serve in slices.

RED VELVET Cake

Deep, dark layers of sponge are covered in creamy white icing
to create this truly impressive cake.

MAKES: 10–12 SLICES

75g unsalted butter, softened
300g caster sugar
2 eggs, beaten
1 teaspoon vanilla extract
225g plain flour
3 tablespoons unsweetened cocoa
   powder
1½ teaspoons bicarbonate of soda
Pinch of salt
1 tablespoon red food colour paste
125ml buttermilk
1 tablespoon white vinegar
FOR THE ICING
75g unsalted butter, softened
225g cream cheese or full-fat soft
   cheese, softened
450g icing sugar
1 teaspoon vanilla extract

1. Preheat the oven to 180°C/350°F/Gas mark 4. Grease and flour two
23cm round sandwich cake tins.

2. For the cake, cream the butter and sugar together in a bowl, then
beat in the eggs and vanilla extract. Sift the flour, cocoa powder,
bicarbonate of soda and salt into a separate bowl. Stir the food colour
paste into the buttermilk.

3. Alternately add the flour and buttermilk mixtures to the creamed
mixture. Stir in the vinegar, mixing well. Pour the mixture into the
prepared tins, dividing it evenly. Bake in the oven for 30–35 minutes, or
until firm to the touch. Cool in the tins for 10 minutes, then turn out
onto a wire rack and leave to cool completely.

4. For the icing, beat the butter and cream cheese or soft cheese
together in a bowl. Beat in the icing sugar and vanilla extract, mixing well.
Sandwich the two cakes together with some icing, then spread the
remaining icing over the top of the cake. Serve in slices.

PRALINE LAYER Cake

Toasted pecan nuts make a truly delicious praline for this tasty layer cake.

MAKES: 8–10 SLICES

115g dark bitter chocolate, broken
  into squares
50g unsalted butter
400g caster sugar
2 egg yolks
125ml milk
200g self-raising flour
Pinch of salt
½ teaspoon bicarbonate of soda
1 teaspoon vanilla extract
200g granulated sugar
50g toasted pecans, chopped
250ml whipping cream

CAKE TIP
*If you don't own a food
processor put the praline
into a strong plastic bag and
crush with a meat mallet or
small hammer, or use a
pestle and mortar.*

1. Preheat the oven to 170°C/325°F/Gas mark 3. Grease and base line two 20cm round sandwich cake tins.

2. Melt the chocolate and butter in a large heat-proof bowl set over a pan of gently simmering water, then remove and cool to room temperature. Stir in the caster sugar. Add the egg yolks and half of the milk and mix well.

3. Add the flour, salt and bicarbonate of soda and beat for 1 minute, then beat in the remaining milk and the vanilla extract. Pour the mixture into the prepared tins, dividing it evenly.

4. Bake in the oven for 25–30 minutes, or until just firm to the touch. Turn out onto a wire rack and leave to cool.

5. Melt the granulated sugar in a heavy-based saucepan over a low heat. Lightly oil a piece of foil on a baking sheet. When the sugar is golden, stir in the pecans. Pour evenly onto the oiled surface. Leave to cool, then break into small pieces. Process in a blender or food processor to form a fine powder.

6. Whip the cream in a bowl to form soft peaks, then fold in the nut powder. Sandwich the two cakes together with some of the cream icing, then spread the remaining icing over the top of the cake. Cover and refrigerate before serving.

STRAWBERRY Cake with Flaked Almonds

This delightful strawberry cake is a great summertime treat. Substitute best-quality strawberry compote in place of the fresh strawberries, if you prefer.

MAKES: 10–12 SLICES

250g unsalted butter, softened
250g caster sugar
2 eggs, beaten
1 teaspoon vanilla extract
Pinch of salt
4 tablespoons soured cream
1 teaspoon bicarbonate of soda
225g plain flour
100g ground almonds

FOR THE ICING
350ml whipping cream
2 tablespoons icing sugar
1 teaspoon finely grated lemon zest
4 tablespoons soured cream
4 tablespoons toasted flaked almonds
450g strawberries, halved and sliced

1. Preheat the oven to 180°C/350°F/Gas mark 4. Grease and base line a deep 23cm round cake tin.

2. For the cake, cream the butter and sugar together in a bowl until pale and fluffy. Gradually add the eggs, beating well after each addition. Stir in the vanilla extract, salt and soured cream.

3. Sift the bicarbonate of soda with the flour, then fold this into the egg mixture together with the ground almonds.

4. Spoon the mixture into the prepared tin and level the surface. Bake in the oven for 30–35 minutes, or until golden and firm to the touch. Turn out onto a wire rack and leave to cool.

5. For the icing, whip the cream in a bowl to form soft peaks. Add the icing sugar, lemon zest and soured cream, mixing well. Spread the icing over the top and sides of the cake. Press the flaked almonds around the sides and arrange the strawberry slices on top of the cake. Refrigerate until ready to serve. Serve in slices.

CHOCOLATE & CHESTNUT MACAROON Cake

Drizzle each slice of this tempting cake with melted dark chocolate before serving, if you like.

MAKES: 6–8 SLICES

300g icing sugar
½ teaspoon bicarbonate of soda
4 large egg whites
200g ground almonds
100g canned sweetened chestnut purée
2 tablespoons maple syrup
75g dark bitter chocolate, melted
250g mascarpone cheese
150ml whipping cream
Chocolate curls, to decorate

1. Preheat the oven to 140°C/275°F/Gas mark 1. Line three baking sheets with non-stick baking paper and draw an 18cm circle on each.

2. Sift the icing sugar and bicarbonate of soda into a bowl. In a separate bowl, whisk the egg whites until stiff. Gradually whisk in three-quarters of the icing sugar until the mixture is stiff and glossy. Mix the remaining icing sugar into the ground almonds, then fold this into the whisked egg whites. Divide the mixture equally between the three circles on the prepared baking sheets and spread out evenly.

3. Bake in the oven for 10 minutes. Reduce the oven temperature to 110°C/225°F/Gas mark ¼ and bake for a further 1¼ hours. Transfer to a wire rack to cool, then peel away the paper.

4. Beat the chestnut purée and maple syrup together in a bowl until smooth. Stir in the melted chocolate, then beat in the mascarpone cheese followed by the cream, mixing well.

5. Place a meringue round on a serving plate and spread with half of the chestnut mixture. Place a second meringue round on top and spread that carefully with the remaining chestnut mixture. Top with the remaining meringue round and sprinkle with chocolate curls to decorate.

DARK CHOCOLATE
Cheesecake

A fabulous cheesecake for chocoholics. Use the best-quality chocolate you can find.

MAKES: 10–12 SLICES

200g digestive biscuits, crushed
50g unsalted butter, melted
675g cream cheese or full-fat soft cheese
Pinch of salt
3 tablespoons cornflour
200g caster sugar
2 eggs, beaten
2 egg yolks
2 teaspoons vanilla extract
350ml whipping cream
125ml soured cream
275g dark bitter chocolate, melted
6 tablespoons unsweetened cocoa powder, sifted, plus extra for dusting
2 tablespoons chocolate shards or curls

1. Preheat the oven to 150°C/300°F/Gas mark 2. Grease a 23cm springform tin fitted with a flat base.

2. In a small bowl, mix together the biscuit crumbs and melted butter, then press this mixture evenly into the base of the prepared tin. Bake in the oven for 10 minutes, or until lightly browned, then remove from the oven and set aside to cool.

3. Beat the cream cheese or soft cheese in a large bowl until smooth. Add the salt, cornflour and sugar and beat together for 1 minute. Gradually add the eggs and egg yolks, beating well to combine. Stir in the vanilla extract. Lightly whip the cream in a separate bowl. Fold the whipped cream and soured cream into the soft cheese mixture.

4. Stir in the melted chocolate and sifted cocoa powder, mixing well. Pour the mixture evenly over the biscuit base in the tin. Bake in the oven for 55–60 minutes, or until set at the edges but slightly soft in the centre. Turn off the oven, but leave the cheesecake inside for 45 minutes.

5. Remove the cheesecake from the oven and cool to room temperature. Remove from the tin, place on a serving plate, cover with foil and refrigerate until cold. Decorate the cheesecake with chocolate shards or curls and dust with extra sifted cocoa powder before serving. Serve in slices.

CLASSIC CHEESECAKE
with Blackberry Topping

A delicious fresh blackberry compote tops a classic baked
cheesecake to create this very tempting dessert.

MAKES: 10–12 SLICES

14 digestive biscuits, crushed
65g unsalted butter, melted
3 large eggs, separated
175g caster sugar
340g cream cheese or full-fat soft
   cheese
200ml soured cream
2 tablespoons cornflour
2 teaspoons vanilla extract
4 teaspoons finely grated lemon zest
FOR THE TOPPING
450g fresh blackberries
100g caster sugar
4 teaspoons arrowroot
4 tablespoons blackberry or cherry
   liqueur

1. Preheat the oven to 180°C/350°F/Gas mark 4. Grease and base line a
23cm springform tin fitted with a flat base. Mix the biscuit crumbs and
melted butter together and press evenly into the base of the prepared tin.

2. Whisk the egg yolks and half of the sugar together in a bowl until
light and fluffy. Gradually add the cream cheese or soft cheese, whisking
until smooth. Add the soured cream, cornflour, vanilla extract, lemon zest
and the remaining sugar and mix well.

3. In a separate bowl, whisk the egg whites until stiff, then fold them
into the soft cheese mixture. Pour the mixture evenly over the biscuit
base in the tin. Bake in the oven for 1–1¼ hours, or until just set and
golden on top. Turn off the oven. Run a knife around the inside edge of
the tin, then leave the cheesecake to cool in the oven with the door ajar.

4. For the topping, put the blackberries in a saucepan with the sugar and
4 tablespoons of water and cook gently for 5 minutes, or until the berries
are soft. Blend the arrowroot with the liqueur and stir into the fruit. Bring
to the boil, then remove from the heat and leave to cool.

5. Remove the cheesecake from the tin and place on a serving plate.
Pour the blackberry mixture evenly over the top. Refrigerate for 4 hours
before serving.

PINEAPPLE UPSIDE-DOWN Cake

CAKE TIP
Use canned or fresh apricot, peach or pear halves instead of pineapple rings if you wish.

This cake will be much loved for its spectacular appearance when served.

MAKES: 8–10 SLICES

50g unsalted butter
100g soft light brown sugar
425g can pineapple rings in natural juice, drained
7 red glacé cherries
50g toasted flaked almonds (optional)
200g caster sugar
3 eggs, separated
5 tablespoons unsweetened pineapple juice
$\frac{1}{2}$ teaspoon vanilla extract
$\frac{1}{4}$ teaspoon almond extract
150g self-raising flour, sifted
1 teaspoon baking powder
$\frac{1}{8}$ teaspoon salt
Evaporated milk or single cream, to serve

1. Preheat the oven to 180°C/350°F/Gas mark 4. Grease and base line a deep 23cm round cake tin. Reserve 15g of the butter, then melt the rest in a saucepan over a low heat. Pour into the prepared tin and sprinkle the brown sugar evenly over it.

2. Arrange the pineapple rings in the butter-sugar mixture, placing a glacé cherry in the centre of each ring. Sprinkle the flaked almonds over the top, if using.

3. Cream the reserved butter and the caster sugar together in a bowl, then gradually beat in the egg yolks. Add the pineapple juice, then the vanilla and almond extracts, mixing well. Sift the flour, baking powder and salt into the creamed mixture and fold in, mixing well.

4. In a separate bowl, whisk the egg whites until stiff, then fold them into the creamed mixture. Spoon the mixture evenly over the pineapple base in the tin.

5. Bake in the oven for 30–35 minutes, or until firm to the touch. Remove the cake from the oven and leave to cool in the tin. Loosen the cake from the tin and invert onto a serving plate so that the pineapple and cherry base is now on top. Serve the cake warm or cold in slices with evaporated milk or single cream.

CHOCOLATE & STRAWBERRY LAYER Cake

A dark chocolate icing complements the sweet fruit filling perfectly in this luxurious chocolate cake. Serve with whipped cream, if you like.

MAKES: 8–10 SLICES

250g dark bitter chocolate, chopped
175ml milk
250g unsalted butter, softened
225g soft dark brown sugar
3 eggs, beaten
200g self-raising flour
1 tablespoon baking powder
4 tablespoons unsweetened cocoa powder
4 tablespoons strawberry compote or strawberry jam
50g icing sugar

1. Preheat the oven to 170°C/325°F/Gas mark 3. Grease and base line two 20cm round sandwich cake tins. Melt 100g of the chocolate and the milk together in a heat-proof bowl set over a pan of simmering water. Remove from the heat and set aside.

2. Using a hand-held electric mixer, cream 125g of the butter and all of the brown sugar together in a bowl until pale and fluffy, then gradually beat in the eggs.

3. Sift the flour, baking powder and cocoa powder into a separate bowl. Add the flour mixture to the creamed mixture alternately with the chocolate milk. Increase the speed of the mixer for about 30 seconds to mix thoroughly.

4. Divide the mixture evenly between the prepared tins and level the surface. Bake in the oven for 25–30 minutes, or until firm to the touch. Turn out onto a wire rack and leave to cool.

5. Melt and cool the remaining chocolate. Sandwich the two cakes together with the strawberry compote or jam. Cream the remaining butter in a bowl, then beat in the icing sugar. Pour in the melted, cooled chocolate and mix well. Spread the chocolate icing over the top of the cake. Serve in slices.

DEVIL'S FOOD CAKE with
Choc-Orange Icing

MAKES: **8–10 SLICES**

175g dark bitter chocolate, broken
    into squares
150g unsalted butter, softened
100g caster sugar
6 large eggs, separated
75g plain flour
50g ground almonds
FOR THE ICING
200ml whipping cream
200g dark bitter chocolate, broken
    into squares
2 teaspoons finely grated orange zest
Sugar orange slices, to decorate
Sifted icing sugar, for dusting
    (optional)

1. Preheat the oven to 180°C/350°F/Gas mark 4. Grease and line a deep 20cm round cake tin.

2. For the cake, melt the chocolate in a heat-proof bowl set over a pan of gently simmering water. Remove and cool slightly. In a separate bowl, beat the butter and half of the sugar together until creamy. Beat in the melted chocolate, then beat in the egg yolks, one at a time.

3. Sift the flour and ground almonds into a separate bowl. In another bowl, whisk the egg whites until stiff, then gradually whisk in the remaining sugar. Stir half of the whisked egg whites into the chocolate mixture to loosen it slightly, then fold in the flour mixture together with the remaining whisked egg whites.

4. Spoon the mixture into the prepared tin and level the surface. Bake in the oven for 50–60 minutes, or until a skewer inserted into the centre comes out clean. Cool in the tin for 10 minutes, then turn out onto a wire rack and leave to cool completely.

5. To make the icing, heat the cream in a saucepan until nearly boiling. Remove the pan from the heat, stir in the chocolate until melted, then stir in the orange zest. Keep stirring until thick. Spread the icing evenly over the top and sides of the cake. Decorate with sugar orange slices, then leave the icing to set before dusting the cake with sifted icing sugar, if you like. Serve in slices.

BLUEBERRY CAKE
with Streusel Topping

MAKES: 8–10 SLICES

600g plain flour
4 teaspoons baking powder
1 teaspoon salt
125g unsalted butter, softened
250g caster sugar
2 eggs, lightly beaten
1½ teaspoons vanilla extract
300ml milk
350g fresh blueberries

FOR THE TOPPING

125g caster sugar
65g soft light brown sugar
125g unsalted butter, softened
100g plain flour
50g toasted walnuts or pecans,
   chopped
1½ teaspoons ground cinnamon
½ teaspoon freshly grated nutmeg
½ teaspoon salt

FOR THE FILLING

350g cream cheese or full-fat soft
   cheese, softened
65g caster sugar
1 egg
Finely grated zest of 1 lemon
1–2 tablespoons fresh lemon juice
1 teaspoon vanilla extract

1. Preheat the oven to 190°C/375°F/Gas mark 5. Generously grease a 33 x 23cm ovenproof glass baking dish.

2. To make the topping, rub the sugars, butter and flour together in a bowl until the mixture forms coarse crumbs. Stir in the nuts, cinnamon, nutmeg and salt. Refrigerate until ready to use.

3. To make the filling, using a hand-held electric mixer, beat the cream cheese or soft cheese in a bowl until creamy. Gradually beat in the sugar. Beat in the egg, lemon zest and juice and vanilla extract. Set aside.

4. For the cake, sift the flour, baking powder and salt into a bowl. Set aside. In a separate bowl, beat the butter until creamy. Gradually beat in the sugar, then beat in the eggs and vanilla extract. Fold in the flour mixture alternately with the milk, mixing well. Fold in the blueberries.

5. Spread a little less than half of the cake mixture over the base of the prepared dish. Gently spread the filling evenly over the cake mixture, then sprinkle a quarter of the topping over the filling. Drop spoonfuls of the remaining cake mixture over the top and spread evenly. Sprinkle the remaining topping over the surface.

6. Bake in the oven for about 1 hour, or until crunchy and golden on top. Transfer to a wire rack and leave to cool. Cut into squares and serve warm or at room temperature.

BLACK CHERRY & CHOCOLATE Cake

CAKE TIP

Use fresh cherries when they are in season instead of glacé cherries for a stylish decoration.

This classic Black Forest gâteau is sure to be a family favourite.

MAKES: 10–12 SLICES

Two 425g cans stoned black cherries, drained
125ml rum
6 eggs
200g caster sugar
150g self-raising flour
5 tablespoons unsweetened cocoa powder
600ml double or whipping cream
3 tablespoons black cherry jam
115g dark bitter chocolate, grated
12 dark red glacé cherries, to decorate

1. Preheat the oven to 200°C/400°F/Gas mark 6. Grease and base line two 23cm round sandwich cake tins. Put the cherries in a bowl and pour over half of the rum. Set aside.

2. Put the eggs and sugar, less 3 tablespoons, in a large heat-proof bowl set over a pan of simmering water. Using a hand-held electric mixer, whisk for 15–20 minutes, or until the mixture is pale, creamy and thick enough to leave a trail Remove from the heat. Sift the flour and cocoa powder over the whisked egg mixture and fold in gently but thoroughly.

3. Pour the mixture into the prepared tins, dividing it evenly. Bake in the oven for 12–15 minutes, or until just firm to the touch. Turn out onto a wire rack and leave to cool.

4. Whip the cream in a bowl to form soft peaks. Whisk in the remaining rum and the 3 tablespoons of sugar. Brush each of the sponge cakes with the rum that the cherries have been soaking in, then spread the jam evenly over one of the sponge cakes. Top this sponge cake with one third of the cream and the cherries. Place the other sponge cake on top, then cover the top of the cake with cream, reserving some for decoration.

5. Sprinkle the top of the cake with the grated chocolate, then pipe 12 rosettes of cream around the top edge of the cake. Top with the glacé cherries. Refrigerate for 45 minutes before serving.

CAPPUCCINO TRUFFLE Cake

This delicious coffee and chocolate combination is more like a cold soufflé than a cake. Serve with whipped cream, if you like.

MAKES: 6–8 SLICES

1 tablespoon instant coffee powder
150ml boiling water
100g ready-to-eat pitted dried prunes, chopped
4 tablespoons Tia Maria, or other coffee liqueur
175g dark bitter chocolate, broken into squares
115g unsalted butter
5 eggs, separated
100g caster sugar
1 teaspoon vanilla extract
1 tablespoon cornflour
Unsweetened cocoa powder, for dusting

1. Dissolve the coffee powder in the boiling water in a small jug, then pour over the prunes in a bowl. Stir in the Tia Maria. Leave to soak overnight.

2. Preheat the oven to 170°C/325°F/Gas mark 3. Grease and line a 20cm springform tin fitted with a flat base.

3. Melt the chocolate and butter in a heat-proof bowl set over a pan of hot water. Remove from the heat.

4. Using a hand-held electric mixer, whisk the egg yolks and sugar together in a separate heat-proof bowl set over a pan of simmering water, until the mixture is very thick and creamy. Remove from the heat.

5. Drain any excess liquid from the prunes. Stir the vanilla extract, drained prunes and melted chocolate into the creamy mixture and set aside.

6. With clean beaters, whisk the egg whites in a clean bowl until stiff. Whisk in the cornflour, then fold this into the chocolate mixture. Pour the mixture evenly into the prepared tin. Bake in the oven for 50 minutes, or until springy to the touch.

7. Remove the cake from the oven and leave it to cool completely in the tin. Turn the cake out onto a serving plate and dust with sifted cocoa powder. Serve in slices.

ICE CREAM Cake

MAKES: 10–12 SLICES

300g caster sugar
150g self-raising flour
8 egg whites
1¼ teaspoons cream of tartar
Pinch of salt
1 teaspoon almond extract
½ teaspoon vanilla extract
6–8 maraschino cherries (optional)
Sifted icing sugar, for dusting
FOR THE MELBA SAUCE & FILLING
150g caster sugar
225g fresh raspberries, puréed and
  chilled
Scoops of ice cream, preferably
  vanilla – to fill the centre recess
425g can peach slices in fruit juice,
  drained

CAKE TIP
*As an alternative, use
mint choc-chip ice cream and
dust the top of the cake with a
combination of sifted icing sugar
and unsweetened cocoa powder.
Serve with fresh strawberries
and a hot chocolate
sauce.*

1. Preheat the oven to 180°C/350°F/Gas mark 4. For the cake, sift the caster sugar twice into a bowl. In a separate bowl, sift the flour four times. Set both aside.

2. Whisk the egg whites in another bowl until frothy. Add the cream of tartar and salt, and continue to whisk until the mixture forms soft peaks. Sprinkle 2 tablespoons of the caster sugar over the egg white peaks and whisk until blended. Repeat the process until the caster sugar is all used up.

3. Whisk in the almond and vanilla extracts. Using a rubber spatula, fold in the flour, 50g at a time. Cut the maraschino cherries into quarters, if using, and fold them into the cake mixture. Spoon the mixture into an ungreased 23cm fluted ring mould. Cut through the mixture with a knife to get rid of any air bubbles, then level the surface. Bake in the oven for 40–60 minutes, or until the top turns light brown.

4. Invert the cake onto a wire rack and leave to cool in the mould for 1 hour. Run a sharp knife around the edges of the mould to loosen the cake before transferring it to a serving plate.

5. Meanwhile, to make the melba sauce, combine the sugar and 125ml boiling water in a saucepan and boil for 10 minutes. Remove the pan from the heat and set aside to cool, then add the raspberry purée. Press the mixture through a fine sieve and refrigerate.

6. To serve, fill the centre recess of the cake with the ice cream and peaches. Pour some of the melba sauce over the ice cream, taking care to avoid soaking the cake, then serve the rest separately. Dust the cake with sifted icing sugar and serve immediately in slices.

MIDDLE EASTERN ORANGE Cake

To flavour this moist and delicious cake, 2 whole oranges, including the pith and peel, are used. This gives it a really intense citrus taste and makes it perfect to serve as a dessert with crème fraîche or whipped cream.

MAKES: 10–12 SLICES

2 small oranges
5 eggs
175g light muscovado sugar
225g ground almonds
50g plain flour
1 teaspoon baking powder
2 tablespoons flaked almonds
Sifted icing sugar, for dusting

1. Put the whole oranges in a saucepan and cover with water. Bring to the boil, then cover and simmer for about 1½ hours, or until the oranges are really soft. Remove the pan from the heat, drain and set aside to cool. Halve the oranges and remove the pips, then purée the oranges in a blender or food processor. Measure 300ml of the pulp and discard the rest.

2. Preheat the oven to 180°C/350°F/Gas mark 4. Grease and line a deep 23cm round cake tin. Using a hand-held electric mixer, whisk the eggs and sugar together in a large heat-proof bowl set over a pan of simmering water until the mixture is pale, creamy and thick enough to leave a trail on the surface when the whisk is lifted. Remove from the heat.

3. Fold the measured orange pulp into the whisked egg mixture, together with the ground almonds, flour and baking powder, mixing well. Pour the mixture evenly into the prepared tin, then scatter the flaked almonds over the top.

4. Bake in the oven for 1 hour, or until a skewer inserted into the centre comes out clean. Cool in the tin for 10 minutes, then turn out onto a wire rack. Dust with sifted icing sugar. Serve warm or cold in slices.

PLUM & AMARETTI
Sponge Cake

Crushed amaretti add an interesting crunch to this traybake and the almond flavour works incredibly well with the plums. Serve with crème fraîche or vanilla ice cream for dessert.

MAKES: 24 SQUARES

175g unsalted butter, softened
175g caster sugar
3 large eggs
175g self-raising flour, sifted
2 teaspoons finely grated lemon zest
1 tablespoon fresh lemon juice
6 plums, halved and stoned
25g amaretti biscuits, coarsely crushed
1 tablespoon demerara sugar, for sprinkling

CAKE TIP
When in season, use greengages instead of plums, or try blackberry and apple to ring the changes.

1. Preheat the oven to 180°C/350°F/Gas mark 4. Grease and line an 28 x 18cm cake tin.

2. Cream the butter and caster sugar together in a bowl until pale and fluffy. Gradually add the eggs, beating well after each addition. Sift the flour over the creamed mixture and fold in together with the lemon zest and juice, mixing well.

3. Spoon the mixture into the prepared tin and level the surface. Arrange the plum halves, cut-side down, over the top, then sprinkle with the crushed amaretti and demerara sugar.

4. Bake in the oven for 45–50 minutes, or until risen and golden. Cool slightly in the tin, then turn out onto a wire rack, invert the cake so that the plums are on top and leave to cool. Serve warm or cold cut into squares or slices.

WHIPPED CREAM
Cheesecake

An exceptionally light and creamy cheesecake that makes a flamboyant centrepiece.

MAKES: 12–14 SLICES

200g digestive biscuits, crushed
50g unsalted butter, melted
675g cream cheese or full-fat soft
  cheese
Pinch of salt
3 tablespoons cornflour
200g caster sugar
2 eggs, beaten
2 egg yolks
2 teaspoons vanilla extract
1 teaspoon seeds from a vanilla pod
  (optional)
600ml whipping cream
Fruit, to decorate

1. Preheat the oven to 150°C/300°F/Gas mark 2. Grease a 23cm springform tin fitted with a flat base. Mix together the biscuit crumbs and melted butter and press evenly into the base of the prepared tin. Bake in the oven for 10 minutes, or until lightly browned. Remove from the oven and set aside to cool.

2. Beat the cream cheese or soft cheese in a large bowl until soft and smooth. Add the salt, cornflour and sugar and beat for 1 minute. Gradually add the eggs and egg yolks, beating well to combine. Stir in the vanilla extract and vanilla seeds, if using.

3. In a separate bowl, whip the cream to form soft peaks, then fold half of the whipped cream into the soft cheese mixture. Refrigerate the remaining cream. Pour the soft cheese mixture evenly over the biscuit base in the tin. Bake in the oven for 50–60 minutes, or until set at the edges but slightly soft in the centre.

4. Turn off the oven, leave the cheesecake inside and leave the door ajar. Cool in the oven for 30 minutes. Remove the cheesecake and cool to room temperature, then remove it from the tin, place on a serving plate, cover with foil and refrigerate until cold.

5. Spread the remaining whipped cream evenly over the top of the cheesecake and decorate with your favourite fruit. Serve in slices.

PEACH Cake

The peach halves in this recipe keep the cake moist and fruity —
ideal for a family dessert, served with cream or ice cream.

MAKES: 10–12 SLICES

175g unsalted butter, softened
175g caster sugar
3 eggs, beaten
200g ground almonds
100g self-raising flour
2 teaspoons vanilla extract
425g can peach halves in fruit juice,
   drained
Sifted icing sugar, to dust

1. Preheat the oven to 180°C/350°F/Gas mark 4. Grease and base line a deep 23cm round cake tin.

2. Cream the butter and caster sugar together in a bowl until pale and fluffy, then gradually add the eggs, beating well after each addition. Stir in the ground almonds, flour and vanilla extract.

3. Spoon the mixture into the prepared tin and level the surface. Arrange the peach halves, cut-side down, over the top.

4. Bake in the oven for 35–40 minutes, or until risen and golden. Cool in the tin for 10 minutes, then turn out onto a wire rack, invert the cake \so that the peaches are on top and leave to cool completely. Dust with the sifted icing sugar. Serve in slices.

SUGAR & SPICE Cake

Warming spices richly flavour this easy-to-prepare cake,
which tastes great as a light dessert served with coffee.

MAKES: 12–14 SLICES

175g unsalted butter, softened
250g soft light brown sugar
2 eggs, beaten
250g plain flour
$\frac{1}{2}$ teaspoon baking powder
1 teaspoon ground cinnamon
$\frac{1}{2}$ teaspoon freshly grated nutmeg
$\frac{1}{2}$ teaspoon ground ginger
Pinch of salt
1–2 tablespoons milk
1 tablespoon demerara sugar

1. Preheat the oven to 180°C/350°F/Gas mark 4. Grease and base line a 900g loaf tin.

2. Beat the butter in a bowl until pale and creamy, then add the soft brown sugar and beat for a further 3–4 minutes. Gradually add the eggs, beating well to mix. Sift the flour, baking powder, cinnamon, nutmeg, ginger and salt over the creamed mixture and fold in, gradually adding the milk at the same time.

3. Pour the mixture evenly into the prepared tin, then sprinkle the demerara sugar over the top. Bake in the oven for 50–55 minutes, or until firm to the touch and a skewer inserted into the centre comes out clean. Cool in the tin for 5 minutes, then turn out onto a wire rack and leave to cool completely. Serve in slices.

CAKE TIP
*This cake can be cut into
slices and frozen so a few
slices can be defrosted
and used as a quick dessert
with fresh fruit and
ice cream.*

YEASTED SOURED CREAM Cake

This tasty loaf cake creates an ideal sweet treat to enjoy after a main course or supper.

MAKES: 12–14 SLICES

1 teaspoon dried yeast granules
125ml warmed water
300g plain flour
5 tablespoons soured cream
75g cream cheese or full-fat soft cheese
150g unsalted butter, melted
100g caster sugar
2 eggs, beaten
2 egg yolks
1 teaspoon ground cinnamon
4 tablespoons flaked almonds
3 tablespoons apricot jam
3 tablespoons icing sugar
1 tablespoon lemon juice

1. Grease a 900g loaf tin. Dissolve the yeast in the warmed water in a large bowl, then stir in 2 tablespoons of the flour. Stand in a warm place for about 10 minutes, or until the yeast starts to froth.

2. Mix the soured cream, cream cheese or soft cheese and melted butter together in a separate bowl, then stir in the caster sugar, eggs and egg yolks. Set aside.

3. When the yeast has started to work, add the remaining flour and the cinnamon to the yeast mixture and stir in. Add the soured cream mixture and mix to form a soft dough. Shape the dough into a ball and place it in an oiled bowl. Cover with a clean damp tea towel and leave to rise in a warm place for about 1 hour, or until doubled in size.

4. Knead the flaked almonds into the dough, then shape the dough into an oblong and place it in the prepared tin. Leave to rise again for 20–30 minutes. Meanwhile, preheat the oven to 190°C/375°F/Gas mark 5.

5. Bake the loaf in the oven for 25–30 minutes, or until golden. Turn out onto a wire rack and leave to cool.

6. Gently heat the apricot jam with 3 tablespoons of water in a small saucepan. Brush the apricot glaze evenly over the top of the loaf cake. In a small bowl, combine the icing sugar and lemon juice, then drizzle the lemon icing evenly over the loaf cake. Serve in slices.

RASPBERRY SOUFFLÉ Gateau

MAKES: 10–12 SLICES

75g unsalted butter, melted
200g digestive biscuits, crushed
150g caster sugar
400g frozen raspberries
1 tablespoon powdered gelatine
300ml whipping cream
3 egg whites
Pinch of cream of tartar
200ml double cream, whipped to
   form soft peaks
200g fresh raspberries
3–4 tablespoons seedless raspberry
   jam, warmed

1. Preheat the oven to 180°C/350°F/Gas mark 4. Grease a 23cm springform tin fitted with a flat base. Combine the melted butter, biscuit crumbs and 50g of the sugar in a bowl. Press the crumb mixture evenly into the base of the prepared tin. Bake in the oven for 10 minutes, then remove from the oven and set aside to cool.

2. Combine the frozen raspberries with 3 tablespoons of water in a pan and simmer gently until the raspberries are soft. Process the mixture in a blender or food processor for 30 seconds, then sieve to remove the seeds.

3. Sprinkle the gelatine over 3 tablespoons of hot water. Dissolve in a heat-proof bowl set over a pan of simmering water. Stir the dissolved gelatine into the raspberry pulp. Set aside.

4. In a separate bowl, whip the whipping cream to form soft peaks, then fold this through the raspberry pulp. In another bowl, whisk the egg whites until soft peaks form. Whisk in the cream of tartar and half of the remaining sugar, then whisk in the remaining sugar until the mixture is thick and glossy.

5. Fold the whisked egg white mixture through the raspberry and cream mixture, then spoon the mixture evenly over the biscuit base in the tin. Chill in the refrigerator for 2–3 hours, or until set, then remove the gateau from the tin and place it on a serving plate.

6. Pipe the whipped double cream decoratively around the top edge of the gateau. Arrange the fresh raspberries in the centre on top and spoon the warmed jam evenly over the raspberries. Serve in slices.

APRICOT FRANGIPANE Cake

This dessert cake has a wonderful consistency and flavour. Combining apricots and almonds is nothing new, but the partnership works so well that it is always worth repeating.

MAKES: 8–10 SLICES

125g unsalted butter or margarine, softened
125g caster sugar
½ teaspoon almond extract
100g plain flour
1 teaspoon baking powder
60g ground almonds
2 eggs
8 fresh ripe apricots, halved and stoned
2 tablespoons apricot jam
30g flaked almonds, to decorate

1. Preheat the oven to 180°C/350°F/Gas mark 4. Grease and base line a 23cm springform tin fitted with a flat base.

2. Cream the butter or margarine and sugar together in a bowl until pale and fluffy. Beat in the almond extract. Set aside. Combine the flour, baking powder and ground almonds in a separate bowl. In another bowl, whisk the eggs until they are pale, creamy and thick.

3. Fold the dry ingredients into the creamed mixture alternately with the whisked eggs. Spoon the mixture into the prepared tin and level the surface, then arrange the apricot halves, cut-side down, over the top.

4. Bake in the oven for 35 minutes, or until risen and golden. Cool in the tin for 10 minutes, then carefully remove the cake from the tin and place it on a wire rack, apricot side uppermost. Cool for a further 10 minutes.

5. Melt the apricot jam with 2 teaspoons of water in a small saucepan over a low heat. Press the mixture through a sieve into a bowl. Brush the top of the warm cake with the apricot glaze, then scatter the flaked almonds on top. Serve warm or cold in slices.

CANDIED FRUIT Cassata

MAKES: 8–10 SLICES

100g plain flour
4 large eggs, separated
100g caster sugar
1 teaspoon vanilla extract
Sifted icing sugar, for dusting

FOR THE CASSATA

6 tablespoons sweet Marsala
500g ricotta cheese
100g icing sugar, sifted
75g plain chocolate, finely chopped
100g mixed glacé fruits, chopped
75g toasted flaked almonds, chopped

1. Preheat the oven to 180°C/350°F/Gas mark 4. Grease and flour two baking sheets. Sift the flour into a bowl and set aside.

2. Using a hand-held electric mixer, whisk the egg yolks and half of the caster sugar together in a large heat-proof bowl set over a pan of simmering water, until the mixture is creamy and very thick. Whisk in the vanilla extract. In a separate bowl, whisk the egg whites until stiff. Whisk in the remaining caster sugar until the meringue mixture is thick and glossy.

3. Use a large metal spoon to gently fold the meringue mixture and then the sifted flour into the whisked egg yolks. Spoon the mixture into a piping bag fitted with a plain 2cm nozzle and quickly pipe 11cm lengths of the mixture in lines on the prepared baking sheets. Dust the tops with sifted icing sugar and bake in the oven for 15–18 minutes, or until pale golden and just firm to the touch. Transfer to a wire rack and leave to cool.

4. To assemble the cassata, line a 1.2 litre soufflé dish with cling film. Use half of the sponge fingers to line the bottom of the prepared dish, cutting them to fit where necessary. Dip these sponge fingers into the Marsala and arrange in the base of the dish. Cut the remaining sponge fingers to fit around the sides, then dip each of these in the Marsala and arrange them around the sides of the dish.

5. Mix together the remaining cassata ingredients and spoon evenly into the dish. Top with any leftover pieces of sponge fingers and drizzle over any remaining Marsala. Cover and refrigerate overnight. Invert the dessert onto a serving plate, dust with sifted icing sugar and serve in slices.

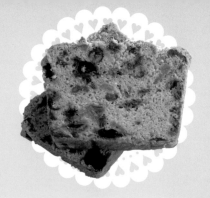

HEALTHY &
SPECIAL DIET
CAKES

PEAR & RASPBERRY Cake

A full and fruity cake, which is best kept in a cool place after baking. The mixture fills the tin before baking but don't worry as it does not rise too much.

MAKES: 12–14 SLICES

- 200g firm pears (2 medium), peeled, cored and chopped
- 150g dried sweetened cranberries
- 225ml raspberry juice or fruits of the forest juice
- 225g mixed fresh raspberries and blueberries
- 150g gluten-free plain flour
- 150g maize flour or fine cornmeal
- 2 teaspoons gluten-free baking powder
- 2 large egg whites
- 175g golden caster sugar
- Sifted golden icing sugar, to decorate (optional)

NUTRITIONAL NOTE
This cake is suitable for low fat, gluten-free, wheat-free, dairy-free and nut-free diets.

1. Preheat the oven to 180°C/350°F/Gas mark 4. Grease and line a 900g loaf tin. Put the pears, cranberries and fruit juice into a saucepan and bring the mixture to the boil over a medium heat. Remove the pan from the heat and set aside to cool.

2. Put the cooled fruit and juice into a large bowl and add the raspberries and blueberries. Sift the plain flour, maize flour or cornmeal and baking powder together and stir into the fruit mixture.

3. In a separate bowl, whisk the egg whites until stiff, then gradually whisk in the caster sugar to make a thick, glossy meringue mixture. Fold a little of the meringue into the fruit mixture to loosen it, then fold in the remainder. Spoon the mixture into the prepared tin and level the surface.

4. Bake in the oven for about 1¼ hours, or until slightly risen, golden brown and firm to the touch. Cool in the tin for about 20 minutes, then turn out onto a wire rack and leave to cool completely. Dust with a little sifted icing sugar, if you like, and serve in slices.

STICKY
Gingerbread

To make this cake even more special, you can make a quick glacé
icing with 150g golden icing sugar and a little warm water and
trickle it over the cake when cold.

MAKES: 16 SQUARES

150g dairy-free margarine
150g dark muscovado sugar
2 large eggs, beaten
125g rice flour
125g potato flour
1 teaspoon bicarbonate of soda
125g black treacle or molasses,
   warmed
125g golden syrup, warmed
1 tablespoon ground ginger
100g raisins
100g preserved stem ginger, drained
   and chopped

1. Preheat the oven to 170°C/325°F/Gas mark 3. Grease and line a deep
20cm square cake tin.

2. Beat the margarine and sugar together in a bowl until creamy.
Gradually add the eggs, beating well after each addition. Add all the
remaining ingredients and beat together until well mixed. Pour the
mixture evenly into the prepared tin.

3. Bake in the oven for 1 hour, then test by inserting a skewer into the
centre – it should come out clean. If the cake needs further cooking,
reduce the oven temperature to 150°C/300°F/Gas mark 2, and bake until
firm. Cool in the tin for about 20 minutes, then turn out onto a wire rack
and leave to cool completely. Cut into slices or squares to serve.

NUTRITIONAL NOTE
This cake is suitable for gluten-
free, wheat-free, dairy-free and
nut-free diets.

SCENTED TEA Loaf

Lady Grey Tea has a lovely scent of orange and lemon peel, but if you can't find it you can substitute Earl Grey Tea. This cake improves with keeping.

MAKES: 12–14 SLICES

150g dairy-free margarine
175g golden caster sugar
250ml strong brewed Lady Grey Tea
250g luxury mixed dried fruit
100g rice flour
100g potato flour
2 teaspoons gluten-free baking
    powder
Finely grated zest and juice of
    1 orange
Finely grated zest of I lemon
1 egg, beaten
2 tablespoons sieved apricot jam,
    warmed

1. Preheat the oven to 180°C/350°F/Gas mark 4. Grease and line a 900g loaf tin.

2. Put the margarine, sugar, tea and dried fruit into a saucepan and bring to the boil. Simmer gently for 5 minutes, stirring occasionally. Remove the pan from the heat and set aside to cool for 15 minutes.

3. Sift the flours and baking powder into a bowl. Add the flour mixture, orange zest and juice, lemon zest and egg to the fruit mixture and stir to mix well. Pour the mixture evenly into the prepared tin.

4. Bake in the oven for 1–1$\frac{1}{2}$ hours, or until well risen and firm to the touch. Remove the cake from the oven and brush the top of the hot cake with the apricot jam.

5. Cool in the tin for about 20 minutes, then turn out onto a wire rack and leave to cool completely. Serve in slices.

NUTRITIONAL NOTE
This cake is suitable for gluten-free, wheat-free, nut-free and dairy-free diets.

CAKE TIP
All gluten-free cakes can be improved by adding $\frac{1}{4}$ teaspoon Xanthum gum to every 100g flour. Readily available from health food shops, it helps increase volume and storage time.

OLIVE OIL Cake

Use an extra-virgin olive oil for this cake but make sure it is a mild
one. This delicious cake is also good served with fresh fruit.

MAKES: 10–12 SLICES

225g golden caster sugar
Finely grated zest of 2 lemons
4 eggs, beaten
175g gluten-free plain flour
2 teaspoons gluten-free baking
   powder
50g ground almonds
5 tablespoons rice milk
150ml mild extra-virgin olive oil
75g dairy-free margarine, melted
Juice of 1 lemon
50g pine nuts, lightly toasted

1. Preheat the oven to 180°C/350°F/Gas mark 4. Grease and line a
23cm springform tin fitted with a flat base.

2. Put the sugar, lemon zest and eggs into a large bowl and whisk
together until the mixture is pale, creamy and thick enough to leave a
trail on the surface when the whisk is lifted. Sift the flour and baking
powder into a separate bowl, then stir in the ground almonds.

3. Whisk the rice milk, olive oil, melted margarine and lemon juice into
the egg mixture, then fold in the flour mixture until just combined. Pour
the mixture evenly into the prepared tin and scatter over the pine nuts.

4. Bake in the oven for 30–40 minutes, or until golden brown and firm to
the touch. Remove the cake from the oven and leave to cool completely
in the tin, then turn out and serve in slices.

NUTRITIONAL NOTE
This cake is suitable for gluten-free, wheat-free and dairy-free diets.

SQUIDGY CHOCOLATE Cake

This tasty cake is very much like a chocolate brownie. You can use pecans or macadamia nuts instead of walnuts or leave them out altogether if you are allergic to nuts.

MAKES: 12–14 SLICES

100g gluten-free plain flour

30g rice flour

4 tablespoons unsweetened cocoa powder

$^1/_4$ teaspoon bicarbonate of soda

$^1/_2$ teaspoon gluten-free baking powder

115g walnuts, chopped

175g dark bitter or plain chocolate, broken into squares

125g dairy-free margarine

4 eggs

300g golden caster sugar

2 teaspoons vanilla extract

FOR THE ICING

125ml coconut milk

125g dark bitter or plain chocolate, chopped

40g dairy-free margarine

25g walnuts, chopped (optional)

NUTRITIONAL NOTE
This cake is suitable for gluten-free, and dairy-free diets.

1. Preheat the oven to 180°C/350°F/Gas mark 4. Grease and line a 23cm round loose-bottomed sandwich cake tin.

2. For the cake, sift the flour, rice flour, cocoa powder, bicarbonate of soda and baking powder into a bowl. Stir in the walnuts. Set aside.

3. Melt the chocolate and margarine together in a heat-proof bowl set over a pan of hot water. Remove from the heat and set aside to cool slightly. In a separate bowl, beat the eggs, sugar and vanilla extract together. Stir in the melted chocolate mixture, then add this to the flour mixture and stir together until just combined.

4. Spoon the mixture into the prepared tin and level the surface. Bake in the oven for about 30 minutes, or until firm to the touch. Remove the cake from the oven and cool in the tin for about 20 minutes, then turn out carefully and place on a serving plate. Set aside to cool completely.

5. To make the icing, put the coconut milk in a small saucepan and bring to the boil. Remove the pan from the heat and immediately add the chocolate and margarine to the hot milk. Stir well until smooth, then leave to cool until the mixture is of a thick spreading consistency. Spread the icing evenly over the top of the cake. Sprinkle with chopped walnuts, if you like, then leave until set. Serve in slices.

ORANGE CAKE
with Rosemary Glaze

This is a tasty cut-and-come-again cake that is good served with tea or coffee.

MAKES: 8–10 SLICES

175g gluten-free plain flour
25g rice flour
¼ teaspoon bicarbonate of soda
¼ teaspoon gluten-free baking
  powder
125g dairy-free margarine
200g unrefined granulated sugar
Finely grated zest of 1 orange
2 eggs, beaten
½ teaspoon vanilla extract
3 tablespoons unsweetened orange
  juice
3 tablespoons rice milk
5 tablespoons coconut milk

FOR THE SYRUP
5 tablespoons unsweetened orange
  juice
30g unrefined golden caster sugar
Sprig of fresh rosemary, washed and
  patted dry

NUTRITIONAL NOTE
This cake is suitable for gluten-
free, and dairy-free diets.

1. Preheat the oven to 180°C/350°F/Gas mark 4. Grease and line a 450g loaf tin. For the cake, sift the flours, bicarbonate of soda and baking powder into a bowl and set aside. In a separate bowl, beat together the margarine, sugar and orange zest. Gradually add the eggs, beating well after each addition.

2. In another bowl, mix together the vanilla extract, orange juice, rice milk and coconut milk. Stir this thoroughly into the egg mixture alternately with the flour mixture. Do not over-mix.

3. Spoon the mixture into the prepared tin and level the surface. Bake in the oven for about 1 hour, or until a skewer inserted into the centre comes out clean.

4. Meanwhile, make the syrup. Put the orange juice and sugar into a small saucepan. Strip the leaves from the sprig of rosemary and add them to the pan. Bring to the boil, stirring, then boil for about 2 minutes, or until syrupy.

5. Remove the cake from the oven. Prick the top of the hot cake all over with a skewer or fork and slowly pour over the syrup. Leave the cake in the tin until completely cold, then turn out and serve in slices.

MANGO & PASSION FRUIT Roll

MAKES: 8–10 SLICES

4 eggs, separated
125g icing sugar, plus extra for
  dusting
1 tablespoon orange flower water
50g rice flour
50g potato flour
1 teaspoon gluten-free baking
  powder

FOR THE FILLING
300ml sheep's or goat's natural
  yoghurt or whipped soya
  topping cream
½ large mango, peeled, stoned and
  chopped
¼ small papaya, peeled, seeded and
  chopped
1 passion fruit

FOR THE DECORATION
½ large mango, peeled, stoned and
  thinly sliced
1 passion fruit, cut in half

NUTRITIONAL NOTE
This cake is suitable for low fat,
wheat-free, gluten-free, nut-free,
and dairy-free diets.

1. Preheat the oven to 190°C/375°F/Gas mark 5. Grease and line a 32 x 22cm Swiss roll tin, then grease the lining paper.

2. For the cake, put the egg whites in a bowl and whisk until the mixture forms soft peaks. Sift half of the icing sugar over the top and whisk in.

3. In a separate bowl, whisk the egg yolks with the remaining icing sugar until the mixture is pale and very thick. Stir in the orange-flower water. Sift the flours and baking powder over the top and fold in. Using a metal spoon, fold in the whisked egg whites mixture, one third at a time.

4. Spoon the mixture into the tin, spreading it evenly. Bake in the oven for about 12–15 minutes, or until springy to the touch. Sprinkle a little extra sifted icing sugar over a large sheet of non-stick baking paper and turn out the sponge cake onto the paper. Remove the lining paper, trim off any firm edges, then loosely roll up the cake with the paper inside and leave to cool on a wire rack.

5. For the filling, carefully unroll the cake and spread the yoghurt or soya cream evenly over the cake. Scatter over the chopped mango and papaya. Halve the passion fruit and spoon the juice and seeds over the fruit.

6. Carefully roll up the cake, place it on a serving plate and dust with extra sifted icing sugar. Decorate with slices of mango and the juice and seeds of the passion fruit. Serve in slices.

FEEL GOOD Cake

This cake is reportedly good for combating menopausal symptoms.
It will keep well for up to 1 week in the refrigerator.

MAKES: 8–10 SLICES

100g soya flour
100g plain wholemeal flour
100g rolled oats
100g linseeds
50g sesame seeds
50g flaked almonds
3 tablespoons sunflower oil
200g dried fruit such as raisins or
   chopped ready-to-eat dried
   apricots or a mixture
1 teaspoon ground cinnamon
1/2 teaspoon ground ginger
Pinch of freshly grated nutmeg
200ml soya milk
1 tablespoon malt extract
2 tablespoons clear honey

1. Preheat the oven to 180°C/350°F/Gas mark 4. Grease and line a 450g loaf tin.

2. Put all of the ingredients into a large bowl and mix together thoroughly. Set aside to soak for 30 minutes. If the mixture is then too stiff, stir in a little more soya milk.

3. Spoon the mixture into the prepared tin and level the surface. Bake in the oven for about 1 1/4 hours, or until a skewer inserted into the centre comes out clean.

4. Cool in the tin for 5–10 minutes, then turn out onto a wire rack and leave to cool completely. This cake is best stored in the refrigerator.

CAKE TIP
Any dried fruit can be used in this cake, try prunes, figs, ready-to-eat sweetened dried blueberries or cranberries, dates, apples and even exotic fruits such as mango or papaya.

ROSEWATER MERINGUE Cake

This meringue is beautifully scented with rosewater and makes a lovely dessert or tea-time treat. The meringue can be made in advance but assemble the cake just before serving.

MAKES: 6–8 SLICES

4 large egg whites
225g caster sugar
2 teaspoons cornflour
1 teaspoon white wine vinegar
A few drops of rosewater essence

FOR THE FILLING & TOPPING
300ml low-fat raspberry or
   strawberry fromage frais
100g fresh strawberries or raspberries
Crystallised rose petals, to decorate

> **NUTRITIONAL NOTE**
> This cake is very low in fat and
> suitable for wheat-free and
> nut-free diets.

1. Preheat the oven to 150°C/300°F/Gas mark 2. Grease two 20cm round sandwich cake tins and line the bases with non-stick baking paper or oiled foil.

2. Whisk the egg whites in a large bowl until the mixture forms soft peaks. Gradually whisk in the sugar a little at a time. Whisk in the cornflour and vinegar and add a few drops of rosewater essence to taste.

3. Spoon the mixture into the prepared tins, dividing it evenly, then level the surface. Bake in the oven for 1½ hours, then turn the oven off and leave the meringues inside until cold.

4. Just before serving, remove the meringues from the tins and peel off the lining paper. Place one meringue round on a serving plate. Spread the fromage frais evenly over the meringue and arrange the strawberries or raspberries on top. Place the second meringue round on top and sprinkle with crystallised rose petals to decorate. Serve immediately, cut into slices.

BERRY LEMON POLENTA Cake

This cake can also be made in a 20cm pie dish and served as a dessert with some yoghurt or whipped soya topping cream.

MAKES: 8–10 SLICES

150g unsalted butter, softened
150g caster sugar
100g ground almonds
80g instant polenta
4 eggs, beaten
Finely grated zest and juice of 1 large
  lemon
1 teaspoon gluten-free baking
  powder
80g raspberries
80g blueberries
Golden caster sugar, for sprinkling

NUTRITIONAL NOTE
This cake is suitable for gluten-free and wheat-free diets.

1. Preheat the oven to 180°C/350°F/Gas mark 4. Grease and base line a 20cm round sandwich cake tin.

2. Beat the butter and sugar together in a bowl until creamy. Add the ground almonds, polenta, eggs, lemon zest and juice and baking powder and mix well. Add the raspberries and blueberries and stir in gently to mix.

3. Spoon the mixture into the prepared tin and level the surface. Bake in the oven for about 40 minutes, or until lightly browned and firm to the touch.

4. Remove the cake from the oven and leave to cool slightly in the tin, then turn out and place on a serving plate. Sprinkle with golden caster sugar and serve slightly warm or cold.

RICH FRUIT Cake

This cake is suitable for those allergic to eggs as well as wheat and dairy.
It will keep for up to 1 week in a cool place or in the refrigerator.

MAKES: 8–10 SLICES

150g sultanas
100g dried apricots, chopped
100g raisins
50g dried prunes, chopped
350g cold mashed pumpkin flesh
2 teaspoons finely grated lemon zest
4 tablespoons sunflower oil
150g soya flour
250g rice flour
1 tablespoon gluten-free baking
 powder
1 teaspoon ground cinnamon
2 teaspoons ground mixed spice

1. Put the sultanas, apricots, raisins and prunes into a saucepan with 500ml of water. Bring to the boil, then remove the pan from the heat and stir in the pumpkin, lemon zest and sunflower oil. Cover and leave until completely cold.

2. Preheat the oven to 170°C/325°F/Gas mark 3. Grease and line a deep 20cm round cake tin. Sift the flours, baking powder and ground spices into a bowl, then stir this into the fruit mixture, mixing well. Spoon the mixture into the prepared tin and level the surface.

3. Bake in the oven for about $1\frac{1}{4}$–$1\frac{1}{2}$ hours, or until firm to the touch. Remove the cake from the oven, cover with foil and leave in the tin until completely cold, then turn out and serve in slices.

NUTRITIONAL NOTE
This cake is suitable for wheat-free, dairy-free, sugar-free, egg-free and nut-free diets.

LIME AND COCONUT Cake

Make this cake in the summer, fill the centre with fresh fruits and serve with iced tea.

MAKES: 16 SLICES

175g dairy-free margarine
175g golden caster sugar
Finely grated zest of 2 limes
4 eggs, separated
100g gluten-free plain flour
100g rice flour
2 teaspoons gluten-free baking
   powder
50g sweetened and tenderised
   desiccated coconut
250ml goat's or sheep's milk natural
   yoghurt

FOR THE ICING & DECORATION

225g icing sugar, sifted
Finely grated zest of 1 lime
About 2 tablespoons freshly squeezed
   lime juice
Toasted flakes of fresh coconut and
   fine strips of lime peel (optional)

1. Preheat the oven to 180°C/350°F/Gas mark 4. Grease a 24cm (1.3 litre) round-bottomed ring tin.

2. Put the margarine, sugar, lime zest and egg yolks in a bowl and beat together until well mixed. Sift the flours and baking powder over the egg yolk mixture and fold in together with the coconut and yoghurt. Mix well.

3. Whisk the egg whites in a separate bowl until soft peaks form. Fold one-third of the whisked egg whites into the cake mixture to loosen it, then fold in the remainder. Spoon the mixture into the prepared tin and level the surface.

4. Bake in the oven for about 30 minutes, or until golden brown and firm to the touch. Cool in the tin for about 10 minutes, then turn out onto a wire rack and leave to cool completely.

5. To make the icing, put the icing sugar in a bowl. Add the grated lime zest, then stir in enough lime juice to make a thick pouring consistency. Pour the icing over the cold cake and decorate with toasted coconut flakes and strips of lime peel, if you like. Serve in slices.

NUTRITIONAL NOTE
This cake is suitable for gluten-free and dairy-free diets.

INDEX

RECIPE CREDITS

VALERIE BARRETT: Pages 24, 28, 31, 32, 39, 44, 49, 64, 68, 72, 75, 80, 84,90, 92, 94, 96, 102, 104, 105, 111, 116, 118, 119, 120, 125, 126, 170, 172, 173, 174, 175, 176, 178, 179, 180, 182, 183, 184.

CAROLINE BARTY: Pages 46, 55, 93.

JENNI FLEETWOOD: Page 79.

MAGGIE MAYHEW: Pages 25, 27, 48, 56, 58, 59, 60, 62, 63, 66, 78,83, 87, 101, 132, 133, 134, 136, 137, 139, 144, 147, 151, 154, 157, 158, 166, 167.

CAROL TENNANT: Pages 42, 43, 82, 100.

PHILIPPA VANSTONE: Pages 22, 26, 30, 34, 35, 36, 38, 40, 50, 54, 65, 69, 70, 71, 76,

86, 98, 99, 108, 110, 112, 114, 115, 122, 124, 128, 140, 142, 143, 146, 150, 153, 160, 161, 162, 163, 164.

LIZ WOLF-COHEN: Pages 74, 138, 152.

SUSAN WOLK: Pages 148, 156.